D — you are
m
 [
I LOVE YOU

Divorce (or Not): A Guide

Part II: (or Not)

~

How to Choose and Use a

Couples Therapist

Joseph Shaub
Attorney at Law
Marriage and Family Therapist

Cover Design by David Moratto

First Volume Edited by Jennifer D. Munro

ISBN-13: 978-1530802265

ISBN-10: 1530802261

Printed in the United States of America by CreateSpace

Who else? To my Beverly

Who taught me how to trust love

We cannot solve our problems with the same thinking we used when we created them.

— Albert Einstein

CONTENTS

Divorce (or Not): A Guide

PART II
(Or Not)

~

How to Choose and Use a Couples Therapist

INTRODUCTION

My mother and father were not well matched. I recall sitting up at night as a small boy listening to them go at it. Things would be thrown, anger vented—I was mystified by the intensity and scared to death. Over years of my own therapy, and later education and training in the field, I came to a greater understanding of the burdens they both carried, and I have made peace with the craziness—but intimate relationships both frightened and fascinated me through most of my young adulthood. In retrospect, it was not a big surprise that I would move into divorce law after trying out a few other specialties, or that I would be strongly drawn to couples therapy upon obtaining my mental health license.

One weekend in the early 2000s, my wife and I travelled down to Portland from Seattle to be regaled for two days by Dr. John Gottman, the preeminent researcher and expert in marital conflict. It might be the most enjoyable educational experience of my life (and I *love* educational experiences). My wife and I absorb information in different ways. I sat there taking notes feverishly, highlighting parts of his handouts, while she used a skinny wooden coffee stirrer to carefully construct intricate geometric designs on page after page of blank paper. She might have retained more than I did. I still recall glancing over at those M.C. Escher-like contraptions with great fondness.

I learned some powerful lessons during those two days. The most important was the revelation that Gottman was training therapists who worked with couples on the brink. He told us that studies revealed that, on average, couples come in for therapy after they have been experiencing serious difficulties for *six years*.

The lesson: Don't expect couples to come into your office with a message that is something like, "Well, we're doing okay, we just need some communication tools." The burdened, the angry, the fearful—these are the people, the truly challenged—that good couples therapy is designed to heal.

The real gift for me was his introduction to the idea that there are professionals out there whose training—whose *calling*—was to help people, who believe they are in failed relationships, repair, and then deepen, those relationships. What a great line of work!

Then a couple of years later, I attended a four-day training, just south of San Francisco, run by Dr. Sue Johnson, a diminutive Canadian fireball of wit, intelligence, and compassion. In the early 1990s, along with Les Greenberg, Johnson had developed an approach to couples therapy that her research demonstrated to be unusually successful. She termed it "Emotionally Focused Therapy." Being a guy, I thought the name she gave her approach, and the book which introduced her thinking to the public, *Hold Me Tight*, were not especially designed to attract males. (If asked, I might have suggested she name her book *Headlocks of Love*.) I'm only semi-serious, here, but what I am dead-on sure about is that her approach to working with couples in pain is incredibly elegant. It is also effective, well thought-out, and has attracted a legion of extremely excited couples therapists to its ranks. While thousands of exceptional couples therapists work from different perspectives, Emotionally Focused Therapy, and the principles of adult attachment from which it stems, inform my own approach. Its influence will be felt throughout these pages.

Relationship books abound. They are probably the second highest selling *genre*, just behind the category that includes such titles as *Moby Dick and the Vampire Harpooners* and *Little Zombie Women*. Self-help books written by the masters of relationship therapy are purchased by lonely, alienated and deeply frustrated spouses by the millions each year, to be read in solitary silence and then pushed into the hands of their partners. This is done in the most ardent hope that a gem will be unearthed in those pages that will open the other's eyes, or heart.

You are not holding that kind of book. As you will hear more than once in the following pages, I believe that couples in distress, when left to their own devices, will probably blow apart (or drift apart—*apart* being the operative word, here). If you are feeling hopeless—if your relationship is failing—I want you to do more than read a book and follow its exercises. I want you to find a good couples therapist and work with that person. This is a book about couples therapists—how the good ones think and work. Bad couples therapy can be dispiriting and painful. Good couples therapy can change your life in ways you can hardly imagine right now.

Of the many therapies that boast legions of committed practitioners, the approach with which I most resonate is Emotionally Focused Couples Therapy (EFT). I will describe in these pages what, *for me*, comprises the essence of EFT and how it supports a distressed couple in healing. While I have been deeply committed to this approach for a number of years, there are many others who have traveled this path far longer than I. These are the trainers and the masters of the craft, who speak with an authority that garners universal respect among practitioners. This book is written with great respect for these therapists[1] and the deepest appreciation for their continuing contributions in blog posts, articles and the EFT therapists' list serve. Finally, it is written in the hope that, should you be struggling in your own bond, you find one of these people, or others trained by them, to support you in your journey. Information about these many gifted professionals can be found in the Appendix.

What follows is a mix of things: insights from some of the deans of couples therapy and suggestions on ways to shift your paradigm and see yourself and your partner in an altogether different light, with occasional spicing by my own idiosyncratic observations of couples in therapy. To begin each chapter, we will visit Cathy and Dennis, who in pretty familiar ways, tick each other off and find themselves driven apart by their conflict. We'll also spend some time with their therapist, Norma, as she works through the challenges of her practice and the joys of helping estranged, frightened and despairing individuals find connection. Each chapter will end with a short list of "Takeaways" that may help focus your own thinking and support you in the task ahead.

You may note that this is a pretty-recent follow up edition to the first publication of the single volume *Divorce (or Not): A Guide*. When I first wrote this guide, putting the discussion of divorce and marital therapy between the same covers seemed natural…to *me*. The dynamics of conflict are identical in many important respects and, based on my own training, it was easy to think of an intimate relationship's trajectory from first meeting to divorce and beyond (if that was to be the outcome) as having far more similarities than differences along its path.

As I discuss in the first volume in this set, *Divorce*, when the decision to end an intimate relationship is made, it invariably arrives after a lengthy period of inner struggle. In the many years I've worked with divorcing people, I have never known anyone who came to the decision lightly. For as much as the divorce-resisting person wishes for a reconsideration of this decision, there is rarely, if ever, a change in the heart of the divorce-pursuer. I realized that a person who picks up a book on how to divorce well has moved beyond a discussion of saving their intimate relationship. Putting these two themes between one cover began to seem discordant and even punishing to the person who had come to a painful, yet inevitable conclusion.

Thus, *Divorce (or Not): A Guide* is now a two volume series. The first, *Divorce,* respects the reality of at least one partner that discussion of reconnection is no longer a viable option. If you *must* divorce, then there are *definitely* ways to approach this task with wisdom, sanity and integrity. The manner that divorce is conventionally (and all-too-commonly) managed in our culture is tragically destructive and there is certainly a better way. While those who are struggling in their current relationship may find this information relevant as they ponder the decision "should I stay or should I go," the converse isn't so true. The person who has decided upon divorce is likely to find a book about how to save that failed relationship more distressing than helpful.

One final thought before we dive in, here. When I sit with a couple during an initial divorce mediation session, I always ask if they had tried couples therapy before throwing in the towel on their relationship. Quite often, the response is, "Yes. We went for a couple of sessions." As you will see from these pages, effective couples therapy is like the proverbial ocean liner. Changing course takes time. Two or three sessions, when you are stressed enough to consider ending the relationship, is usually going to be woefully ineffective. However, a commitment to a *course* of couples treatment can change the trajectory of your relationship and your lives. This book shows you one person's perspective on how it can be done.

CHAPTER 1

The Nature of Conflict

Cathy and Dennis

(*Thursday evening, 6:30 p.m.*) "Goddamn traffic," Dennis thinks to himself as he inches forward in the Arrivals lane at the airport. He's picking up his college roommate and oldest friend, Gabe, for a hungrily awaited weekend visit. They haven't seen each other in two years and a lot has happened since they had a long guy's weekend at Gabe's place in Chicago. Dennis has already texted Gabe to tell him to cool his heels, traffic is a bitch, and he may not get there for another fifteen minutes. His foul mood lifts as he cranks up a classic Springsteen CD and settles in for the traffic crawl. Moments later, the phone rings. He sees it's from home, and his gut tightens. He hits the Bluetooth button on his steering wheel.

"Yup? What's up?"

"When do you think you'll be home?" comes Cathy's questioning voice.

"Traffic sucks," Dennis replies, rubbing his eyes as the brake lights ahead cut and the crawl resumes. "I don't think I'll get to Arrivals for another ten minutes."

"What? Seriously?" squawks Cathy through his speakers. ("Here it comes," he thinks.) "When did you leave the office? We have reservations at Cormier's at seven. We're never going to make it now. You know how impossible it is to get in there!"

"Jesus, relax, will you? If Cormier's doesn't work out, we can go somewhere else. We can sit around and eat hamburgers at home for all I care. I haven't seen Gabe in two years."

"Yes, just like you," is Cathy's response. "You don't care if we go anywhere. You don't care if we have plans or not. It's always about you. I was looking forward to Cormier's for three weeks. If you can't get your ass out of your chair and to the airport on time, I'll call Mary Jane and go with her. You and your friend can have hamburgers or whatever the hell you want."

"Are you crazy?" Dennis feels his heart start to race. "Are you seriously going to wreck this weekend before it gets started? Goddammit," he explodes as he punches his brakes to avoid plowing into the short-stopping Humvee in front of him. "You know, when was the last time you didn't get pissy when I wanted to be with someone else? My God, you are needy."

Stung, Cathy spits back, "Go ahead, be with your holy friend you never see. I'm spending the weekend with Mary Jane." She cuts the connection.

"I cannot believe this," Dennis says to himself as he inches toward a soured rendezvous with his old friend...

(*Thursday evening, 6:30 p.m.*) Cathy sits down to refresh her makeup after spending the last fifteen minutes deciding what to wear for dinner. Things have been tense at home, and she is looking forward to a respite from all that. They made reservations for Cormier's and she can't remember when they had last splurged on a high-end dinner out. Money has been tight since the nursing agency cut back her hours, and Dennis's income from his law practice took a hit this past year. She hasn't seen his good friend, Gabe, for at least seven or eight years, but she remembers liking him very much and Dennis has been truly looking forward to the weekend. There had been fewer negative, snarky comments from him. Mary Jane had told her that Dennis was a "narcissist," and maybe he was and maybe he wasn't, but he sure hadn't been pleasant to be around. She was tired of walking on eggshells around him. He didn't touch her anymore and, the way he had been acting, she was beginning to think he might hate her. Cathy knew that was a pretty strong word, but, in truth, she worried about that. As she applied her eyeliner, she felt a tightness in her chest. She felt so…discardable by Dennis. The excited anticipation that had filled her only minutes before gave way to a dark, resentful emptiness.

Cathy decided to give Dennis a call. He and Gabe should be on their way home to pick her up. They'd be laughing and, while Dennis never seemed to be in a good mood around her, he always was upbeat around his wide circle of friends. She picked up the cell phone and apprehensively, hopefully, said into the speaker, "Call Dennis."

WHY CONFLICT IS SO HARD

"I'm conflict avoidant." *A trial lawyer in marital therapy.*

Most of us approach conflict with trepidation. That's particularly true with intimate conflict. However, life without conflict is impossible unless you wall yourself off in a cave and eliminate human contact. We are, thankfully, not clones of one another, and each person has a unique history, genetic signature, and set of needs and aversions. There will be countless times when these needs and aversions are incompatible with those of someone else in our lives. It may be with our lover who spends too much time in his own pursuits, leaving us feeling ignored. It may be with friends when they want pizza and we want to go to a Mexican joint for dinner. Perhaps our teenage daughter wants to stay out past one o'clock, but we have set a curfew of eleven o'clock. It may be like the couple in the movie, *Annie Hall*, who disagree about their sex life: Annie tells her therapist they have sex "constantly—three times a week," and Woody Allen's character, Alvy, complains to *his* therapist that they have sex "hardly ever—three times a week." Of course, these examples are seemingly endless.

When facing such conflicts, we have a natural, and often mistaken, tendency to believe that we are right and they are wrong. Another way of putting it is, "If they are right, I must be wrong." What is usually the case, though, is that both people are right. Yet, each one believes that satisfying the other person's needs will deprive themselves of important interests they require. It's known as the "fixed pie" approach to conflict—every win for you is a loss for me. So, if any conflict is seen as a potential loss, there is no wonder that many people will try to avoid conflict.

This is an approach to conflict that may be symbolized by two rams butting heads. They smash into each other with such ferocity that their hind legs lift off the ground. In the human, emotional, equivalent, I respond to your statement of your position with a forceful disquisition of my own...to which you reply with a repetition of your points. These fall on my deaf ears which are closed by the frustration and annoyance of feeling *completely unheard*, so I repeat myself to make sure I have been clear. You, in turn, feel that my repeated assertions of a position *you just listened to* only proves that I am not listening to you, so you become angrier and, then, go on to repeat *yourself*. And round and round it goes. This inevitably results in two exhausted, frustrated people who feel profoundly disregarded. Such conflict leads to our alienation from one another. We are left bruised, dismissed and alone. Who would sign up for that?

Yet, there is another, probably more pressing, reason people wish to avoid conflict. That reason is buried in the mists of our memories, for the way conflict was handled by our families of origin will have a profound impact on how we approach conflict in our lives now. The array of exposures to conflict in families is quite wide.

Following are the most common reactions to conflict:

Bury It: Many of us have no real memory of experiencing conflict in our families of origin. Mother and Father made a point of smoothing over any possible disagreement and, if it needed to be aired, this was done away from the kids. We grew up believing that close relationships meant there was no conflict. If we had siblings and we fought with them, these outbursts were frowned upon. Without a model for actual, healthy conflict, we are more inclined to adopt the mistaken belief that conflict must be painful and is to be avoided.

Go For It: Some of us grow up in families that are loud, boister-ous, and full of conflict. Hardly anything gets buried; you learn early to "stand your ground," and, if you are pushed, you push back. Be-cause overt, unchecked conflict can escalate, there is an ongoing risk that the verbal sparring will heat up to the point that things are said that can't be taken back and wounds will be inflicted that may take a long time to heal—if they do at all. Since conflict is part of the back-ground noise in such a family, there might be difficulty knowing what's important and what's not—just as conflict avoiders don't dis-criminate between the critical and the mundane in this arena.

Dominate: Conflicts in families with significant power differen-tials can become damaging if the powerful member needs to maintain his position. Of course, in virtually every family there is a power dif-ferential between parents and children. The same might also be true between partners. When a conflict seems to become a battle for dom-inance by one, there can be an element of psychic survival that gets injected. This person will go for broke and, if they need to threaten or dismantle the other person to achieve their domination, they will not hesitate. Those who grow up in families with one or more people needing to dominate will develop a deep fear of conflict, as old mem-ories of emotionally disabling wounds will continually surface. As adults, we will develop our own survival mechanism, as conflict might set off internal dialogues that are deeply painful. Thus, we will either adopt a domineering mode ourselves to stifle conflict or with-draw habitually for safety.

Get Overwhelmed: Those raised in homes affected by an adult's mental illness or alcohol/drug addiction are usually the least equipped to deal with conflict in their adult lives. While by no means universal, the absence of behavioral boundaries we see in people so afflicted will cause children exposed to conflict in these families to experience distinct trauma. The anxiety experienced by the prospect of conflict can be so overwhelming that any manner of post-traumatic stressful reactions might emerge. While others might be undone by their con-fusion about how to deal with conflict, children of traumatic conflict will need time, compassion, and therapeutic work with an expert in trauma to begin to unravel the painful strictures that bind them when conflict arises in their lives. However, at the same time, because they didn't witness respect for boundaries in these early conflicts, these people might lash out angrily and brutally, making them unsympathetic and even frightening. Any chance at compassion gives way to self-protection.

Find the Logical Solution: This is a (generally unattainable) dream of many people facing intimate conflict. Emotions become hot and they think, "If only we can discuss this logically, we can get this problem resolved." It is at times possible that both people can step back from their emotional reactivity to engage in a dispassionate problem-solving session. In order to pull this off, though, you will need a partner who is equally capable of distancing themselves from their inner cauldron, *and* the issue under discussion can't push either person's hot button. Thus, logical resolution of intimate differences is usually an unrealistic expectation. Even the seemingly logical, "reasonable" person is beset by strong feelings that they are trying to control...with their logic. That's why their partners often feel condescended to, because one person is stirred up while the other appears unaffected emotionally, as they try to control a potentially chaotic exchange, the prospect of which frightens them.

Air It Out and Let It Go*:* People can be pissed or hurt or frightened and can let the other person know it. The key is that both individuals are able to keep the relationship as the Number One priority during any conflict. Each person knows when the exchange is escalating and when to ease back. Also, each person knows that there will be times in any intimate relationship when they will step on each other's toes, and, when our partner yells, "Ouch," it is not a statement of our own inadequacy or a threat that love will be withdrawn. With this understanding, people are able to blow and let it go.

What ties all of these people together is that *intimate* conflict will stimulate our most vulnerable feelings—be they fear or sadness or shame. We are human and all of these feelings reside inside us to one degree or another. Most of us are able to spend our lives protecting ourselves from exposing these vulnerable feelings. Yet when we are face-to-face with our spouse or partner, these carefully hidden inner experiences are most likely to surface. (When they are augmented by the loss, betrayal, and sense of failure that accompanies divorce, it is no wonder that such conflict might feel particularly threatening.) Yet, even if this type of conflict feels like tip-toeing through a field of land mines, it does not have to be painful, counter-productive, or destructive. It could, instead, be enhancing, productive, and healing.

WHAT WE'VE LEARNED
ABOUT INTIMATE CONFLICT

While the name of University of Washington's Dr. John Gott-man is widely known and respected among couples therapists, he did not go into the field with aspirations to be a couples therapist. He was a scientist and researcher (having studied mathematics in college and grad school before getting his PhD in psychology *and* mathematics). For years now, Gottman has observed thousands of couples interact-ing. He has hooked them up to monitors to measure their heart rates, respiration, perspiration, and other stress responses (I imagine him barking, "Okay, stop fighting so we can draw blood!"). He has stud-ied thousands of recordings: of couples who are well bonded and get-ting along; of long and strongly connected people fighting; and of highly conflicted and troubled couples having a range of interactions, from, "Please turn off the lights" to screaming at each other. Years ago, Gottman and his associates set up a condo overlooking a pictur-esque waterway in Seattle that separates the two lakes that define the city (okay, there's the mountains and the Space Needle and the occa-sional rain, too), where couples he was studying would spend a week-end. These couples were asked to do what they do on a day-in, day-out basis in Gottman's "Love Lab," which was equipped with camer-as and microphones in every room except the bedroom and bathroom. Gottman and his associates would watch people say a full range of things, like: *That tie brings out the blue in your eyes. What do you want to do tonight? Can I have the sports page? Fuck you, I want a divorce.* From these observations of the gamut of intimate communi-cation, Gottman was able to formulate powerful insights about con-flict. (While Gottman primarily studied intact couples, his observa-tions about conflict hold true for divorced and divorcing couples as well.)

First and foremost, he observed that conflict is not bad. All cou-ples have their fair share of conflict, and it in no way means that there is a flaw in the relationship. What *is* a problem is mutually escalating conflict. *Many* is the individual who tries to tell her partner something she desperately needs the other person to hear and understand, only to have the response be angry or defensive, triggering an angry retort, only to have the other jab back…etc.

There are a handful of reasons this mutual escalation gets started, but once a couple begins to spin, the exchange can start to ping-pong so fast, so quickly, that each person can become physiologically and emotionally overwhelmed. If allowed to continue and repeat itself for months and years, this pattern will result in exhaustion and disengagement. What each person will also begin to experience from their partner is one of the "Four Horsemen,"[2] the term coined by Gottman to convey how deeply damaging these attitudes and behaviors are to any relationship.

When conflict becomes chronic and each person feels they are getting no relief despite repeated attempts to let their partner in on how hard this all is on them, the complaints shift and become personal. I stop talking about what you are or aren't doing and shift to who *you are* as a person. Complaints morph into *criticism,* the first of Gottman's horsemen. Since many of us grew up in homes rife with criticism—often directed at our little heads—we are sensitized to being spoken to (and of) in that way. There is an automatic reaction with almost all of us and that is *defensiveness*, horseman number two.

It's remarkable how quickly and naturally we move into defensiveness—but then, why not? We are being told by someone close to us (who says they know us well) that there is something wrong with us. We are blamed for another's unhappiness. We think we are expected to feel bad about ourselves and should somehow change our behavior. Who wants to feel blamed for another's unhappiness, *especially when they are only talking about one part of the problem?* We want to set the record straight: "I'm not as bad as you think, and here's why. I'll admit my faults, but I'm not the only one to blame, here!" So we tell our complaining partner why they are wrong or aren't being honest. Sometimes we try to dampen the heat of our partner's anger by trying to move the discussion onto a more rational plane—and they get even angrier at us, accusing us of being "condescending." So we respond with defensiveness tinged with our own anger.

Is this what the first person is longing to hear when they first utter their complaints? Hardly likely. Their anger and frustration will usually get amped up to another level. To which, our defensiveness will follow suit. At this point (if not sooner) the second, and much more corrosive, pair of horsemen arrive. The criticism turns into *contempt*—with its message of superiority. Gottman has said that contempt is the most damaging to a relationship, and the wounds that are inflicted while in the throes of this attitude are often deep and lasting. To imagine that this person, who at one point in the past was a safe haven for us, is now speaking to us with contempt is a switch that is impossible to fathom or process. The experience is overwhelming and distressing. In order to protect ourselves from this seeming onslaught, we must erect high and thick emotional walls *and fast*. This results in the final horseman, which is *stonewalling*. You are done. You are gone. You are unreachable.

One of the great truisms of intimate conflict is that, in our own distress, we completely lose touch with the reality that our behavior is causing equal distress to our partner. Each person is so intensely preoccupied with self-protection (and understandably so) that this behavior is pinching a raw nerve in the other. The *Stonewaller,* who needs to protect himself from the anger, criticism, and growing contempt of his partner, doesn't comprehend in his heightened reactive state that his stonewalling is freaking his partner out. After all, the first has been trying to make a connection, to solve a problem (however imperfectly), and the *Stonewaller* has now completely and totally gone away. The criticizer thinks that all she is trying to do is explain—even if what she's trying to explain is how angry he makes her. She doesn't understand that for most people on the receiving end of this criticism, the pain and confusion and need to defend oneself are intense and automatic.

It's like a dance in which the partners join hands and start to spin in a circle that turns faster and faster, driving them farther apart with psychological centrifugal force. One person feeds on the other and that other feeds on the first, like an atomic chain reaction run amok. It is the bane of a struggling intact marriage and surely more prevalent and troubling when the marriage is ruptured. It's as if the partners let go of each other's hands, and the force of their spinning shoots them both into space. This is post-separation conflict at its most painful. Yet anywhere along the trajectory—from mutual irritation to escalated contempt and stonewalling—this cycle of conflict can be managed and the trajectory altered.

MANAGING THE CYCLE OF CONFLICT

The first step is to understand the *process*. (Get ready, because we are going to talk *a lot* about process in the course of this book.) Conflict is a process of interaction between two people who need the other to at least hear and understand their distress. The subject of most conflict (the thing you're fighting about) is overblown in people's minds. We get so wrapped up in our upset that we lose sight of the fact that we are bouncing off each other and getting more amped and more distressed. So the first step is to just see what is happening through a *process lens*. Good couples therapists have this lens in place, from years of education and experience.

The second step, once you understand and appreciate that your deeply upset feelings are part of this uncontrolled chain reaction, is to move the control rods back into place. What are these? Well, the first is the simple, straightforward decision to *stop*. Take a breath. Disengage and gather your senses again. Tell the other person you need to stop—that you need a time out. This might be hard for you to hear if the person with whom you are intensely engaged in conflict suddenly says they want to *stop* before you feel remotely resolved about what has been upsetting you. It feels like this other person pushed you out to the end of a very high limb and then just sawed the limb off. "How can he cut me off like this and leave me floating? That's typical of the kind of disrespect he shows me!" It is hard to take that breath and come to the realization that neither of you are in any condition to productively resolve what you are trying to talk about right now. Gottman, with all his measurements of heart rate, respiration, perspiration and such, showed that we get so *physiologically* aroused during high conflict that we become "flooded" and incapable of thinking or acting from any other than a frightened, confused place.

The third step is, once you are able to stop, that you agree to address the problem again soon. If either (or both) of you need to sleep on it or have a day or two to gather yourself, then you've got to do it. However, the other person almost always needs some assurance that the question will be addressed again, relatively soon, so he won't feel abruptly cut off. Usually, the way you both react to the issue in question (or to each other) makes it nearly impossible to resolve things yourselves. That's when the assistance of a third person can make all the difference. If you want to preserve the relationship, then a couples therapist might be that third person.

THE COUPLES THERAPIST AS "PROCESS CONSULTANT"

Many years ago, Dr. Sue Johnson observed that process consultant may be the foremost role occupied by the couples therapist. That is only one of the many insights she has provided that underscore the value of the therapist's function. It might be useful, then, to think of the couples therapist as a professional who can stand (or sit) outside the cycle of distress and point out that there is something going on other than what you are fighting about. This requires a paradigm shift for each individual, not unlike the perspective provided by training in "mindfulness."

The essence of mindfulness includes the understanding that you are not your emotions. Oh my goodness, though, when you are smack in the middle of that adrenal surge, such a notion is just *inconceivable*. Perhaps this stems from our childhood experience, when our feelings were denied or criticized. You may be familiar with messages like, "There's nothing to be mad about," or "If you don't stop crying, I'll *really* give you something to cry about!" When showered with these parental proscriptions, we will usually embrace and protect our feelings as vital, legitimate and worthy of recognition. To give up our anger feels like a *surrender of our self*. After all, we usually don't say "I *feel* anger," but rather, "I *am* angry." When told our sadness or fear or anger must end, we will stop the outward expression of these emotions, but grasp them ever more tightly within. Thus, it may feel like a heavy lift to dis-identify with our turbulent emotions.

A different, and helpful, way of thinking about emotions is to appreciate that our particular reaction to a stimulus (Our partner is going to make us late, *again*...She wants to spend money on a treat for herself when she *knows* we are on a budget...He doesn't make any contact during the long workdays, claiming that he is just too busy to come up for air, much less send us a text) is not universal. Not *everybody* would react as we have. That certainly doesn't make our emotional reaction wrong. Rather, this anger, or fear, or contemptuous dismissal is an excellent clue to our inner experience. When we flip out, for example, because we are going to be late due to our partner's dawdling, what do we think he is saying to us by his actions? Is this proof that he doesn't care about what we have told him is important to us *for the thousandth time*? Do we mean that little to him? Or, are we embarrassed that we are with someone so lax? Do we become angry? Ashamed? Frightened? Sad? Frustrated? (It is a good bet that many would answer "frustrated." That seems to be a popular catch-all for a host of unpleasant feelings. If that is the answer, I would suggest one more shot at getting to the more basic, evocative, emotional experience.) Many will dismiss the tardiness as no big deal. Why do we react the way we do? What is it about our makeup, our life experience, and temperament which, together, cause us to have a particular emotional experience in the moment? This exploration is a voyage of self-discovery and never a platform for self-criticism. Whenever we ask ourselves, with real curiosity, "Why did I react in that way?" we are honoring ourselves and our inner lives. Almost always, there are ancient wounds which have been covered by years of life experience and the drifting sands of denial and compartmentalization.[3] These create the "raw spots" in our psyches, as described by Sue Johnson.

How can we develop that perspective? Many mindfulness meditation experiences invite us to imagine our inner world—our mind, if you will—as a placid sea. A feeling or thought will roll across its surface as a wave, and then ebb. Emotions begin to recede as statements of identity. If an individual has great difficulty dis-identifying with their feelings, there is a very strong likelihood that past (usually early) wounds have caused them to lock a death grip around these very intense emotions. This is not a sign of a personal flaw. It is, rather, an indication of pain and a likely violation of that most exquisite need for personal attachment—to be *seen* by a caring and attuned other—of which we'll hear more, later. (An excellent approach to individual therapy for people who struggle with this hurricane of powerful emotions that constantly explode over our inner sea is Dialectical Behavioral Therapy, which utilizes mindfulness as a powerful tool for gaining control of these inner tempests.) This exploration may be very difficult to pursue on our own.

In acting in this role as a process consultant in my office, I have often asked a person why they think they reacted with such intensity in a particular situation. The answer is almost never at the surface of their consciousness, so the initial response is usually, "I don't know." I laugh and tell them my office is a No *"I Don't Know"* Zone, as I gently, and sometimes playfully, wonder what could be underneath that "I don't know." Sue Johnson encourages therapists to provide "empathic reflection and speculation," which suggests to the struggling individual what may be going on underneath their spike of anger or defensive justification. Perhaps it is a gnawing loneliness, a fear of not measuring up, or a number of other vulnerabilities which we hide away from the world (and often ourselves).

Seen in this light, the therapist is a partner in exploration. The suggestions are not to be taken as some wise, unerring insight that is the expert's offer of the truth. Rather, it may be better seen as a suggestion. Do you resonate with the proffered notion ("Betsy, you sound angry at Tom, but I'm wondering if there is also some fear underneath there that you will be left "high and dry" if he abandons you, as you said last week.") or does it leave you flat? Nobody can know what is going on inside you better than you do. A therapist's role is not to tell you who you are but to let your experience unfold in a respectful, safe environment in a process of self-discovery and acknowledgment.

Another part of process which is always present with a struggling couple is the cycle of conflict *between* them. It is almost always the case that once this *process* gets going—the more John does X, the more Mary will do Y and the more Mary does Y, the more John will do X—they will spin faster and faster. Almost certainly, John and

Mary will be so wrapped up in the content of their fight, that they will be blind to this underlying process.

Imagine a fight sounding something like this: Mary complains, "I hate that you flirted with that waitress!" John, defensive and annoyed, responds, "I did not do that." Mary, now getting angrier at being dismissed, spits back, "You think I'm blind? I'm not crazy, you know." John, self-righteously hits back with, "Maybe you *are* crazy, because that's *not* what I was doing." The therapist who refuses to act as a referee, but instead comments on the cycle of mutual reactivity and emotional escalation she just observed, is acting as a *process consultant*.

So, a therapist can act as a process consultant, not only for each person's *internal* process but also for the couple's *interpersonal* process as well.

USUALLY YOU'RE BOTH RIGHT

Of all John Gottman's observations, perhaps my favorite is that 69% of conflicts between intimate partners are perpetual. This applies to people in their first year of marriage and is equally true for the couple who has been together for 60 years and they, and everybody who has known them, say they are a wonderfully bonded pair. We are who we are—and we are who we are *for a reason*. So many intimate conflicts arise from each person trying to get the other to understand and accept our view of the world. That's not to accept it *for themselves*, but just to accept that it is our view and it's legitimate. Couples who get into fights because one person is tight with money and the other wants to spend more freely, or one believes that children should be carefully guided and the other is firm that children need to learn by their own mistakes, or one's idea of a great vacation is to go, go, go and the other's dream is to plant and read are well-advised to understand this *69% Rule*. I cannot count the times in my office that tension evaporates when two people recognize that the other person's being right doesn't mean they must be wrong. Horns unlock; bodies relax; adrenaline is saved for better uses.

Another way to describe this insight is the need to understand the difference between conflict over "interests" and conflict over "positions." A wonderful illustration of this is found in the Fisher, Ury and

Patton's classic, *Getting to Yes.*[4] Two children are fighting over an orange. "I need this orange," each says, staking out their position. Ultimately, they agree, with mom's help, to split the orange in half. Each will be partially satisfied and partially dissatisfied. However, if they had discussed their interests, each would have learned that one needed the rind for cake icing and the other needed the pulp for juice. An apparent conflict could have been easily resolved with a sharing of interests. It has long been accepted by conflict resolution professionals that positional conflicts are harder to resolve. Unfortunately, when the stakes are experienced as high, people are more apt to take positions. Intimate conflict tugs at our deepest needs and fears. The stakes always feel particularly high when we find ourselves going toe-to-toe with our lover.

(If you are seriously considering ending your relationship, it is important to understand that divorce conflicts are almost always experienced as particularly challenging, when children and future financial security are in the mix. Thus, we make a natural shift to dug-in positional bargaining when confronted with divorce conflict.

A dad wakes up in the same house as his kids every day. He might be involved in their morning routine or he might not. Still and all, this is his family and, whatever else he does, it serves as an anchor. While the numbers are shifting, most dads still let the mom handle the parenting details by default. I recall my wife taking a three-week trip with her best friend for her friend's fiftieth birthday. I got to be with our ten-year-old daughter during those wonderful days. I handled it all without problem (other than being told every day, "You don't make sandwiches as good as Mom!"). It was a sweet experience and I relish the memory. When her mom returned, things slid back to the old regular way. If we had gotten divorced around that time, I would have ended up with less time with our daughter than I wanted (needed), even if it had been an equal time share with her mom. Usually, that's not how it works, as the parent who has had primary responsibility for parenting will often continue in that role. Thus, many fathers end up feeling that they have lost their family. It is a grievous loss. Moms experience great loss around parenting as well. For many women, parenting is the most important role they have in life. It is a blessed and honored role. When a marriage ends, there will be a hole in the mother's heart for those times her children are away with their other parent—even when mom and dad get along. Both people feel an enormous loss, but when they try to convey this to the other, all they get in return is *that other person's* loss, coupled with resentment that *their* loss doesn't seem important to the other. If they end up arguing over days and hours of time, their *positional* conflict will run them right up against a wall.

The same person who has to leave the home to work, day in and day out over the years, might feel the pride of being able to provide for a family he gets less time with than he'd wish. These are the sacrifices he makes, but they might seem less so as he excels in his work and feels embedded in the culture of the job. His efforts put money in the family checking account, and the growing pension is a testament to this work. These are *his* hours and *his* efforts. When the bonds of the marriage unravel and snap, he wonders what the heck he was spending all that time *doing* during those years. It becomes hard to wrap his head around having to share the pension he labored for. Even more acutely, the partner who put any thoughts of her own career aside, based on the implicit belief that they were a team, is suddenly facing a future of diminished prospects and impending want. How will she be able to manage financially? As both people experience their standard of living critically jeopardized, he wonders how he'll manage all those nights eating take-out food alone and wants to conserve what he *does* earn; she hears him suggest through his own fear of loss that maybe she should get a job doing what she last did twelve years ago, and she is mystified that he would even think such a thing.

It is over money worries and loss of parenting/family time that anxiety spikes and worries prevail during divorce conflict. Views narrow and positions are taken. Lawyers fuel these positions by advising each person what he or she is "entitled to" under the law.

In making this most wrenching of all decisions, it might be helpful to consider the realities of divorce, which are described in the first book of this set, *Divorce*.)

The paradigm shift for couples in high distress is like the ocean liner mentioned in the Introduction. We enter the first meeting with a couples therapist invariably worried we will be the one blamed for the discord and distance, while at the same time hoping that this third person "expert" can get our partner to finally see *their* part. "I'll take my part of the blame, but not the whole lot. The blame has to be shared," is the line in the sand drawn by each person as they settle into the therapist's office.

How does the couples therapist shift these two wounded and struggling people away from blame (and shame) and into a more productive and healing mindset? That is the subject of the following chapters.

TAKEAWAYS

- **Conflict is natural and part of life. It's not "that" you have conflict that is a problem. It is "how" you have conflict.**

- **Every position taken in a conflict has underlying needs and interests that are usually understandable and can be appreciated by the other person. Sit quietly alone with a pad and pen and draw a line down the middle of the page. On the left, list your positions, and on the right, think about what needs and interests you have. For example, on the left might be, "You spend too much money," and on the right might be, "I worry we might run out of money," or, "There are things I want to do that I don't because I don't think we have the money. I feel deprived when I see that you spend money on things you want." See if you can couch these needs in statements about yourself rather than the other person. Does this build a platform that allows you to have a different conversation about what separates you on a particular topic? Like most of us, you may need help engaging in this sensitive conversation.**

- **Talk to your partner about how upset you both can get in the midst of a conflict and your need to take a break sometimes to settle down physiologically. Work out your own joint code for stopping for a time. It can be simple: "I need to take a break," or, "Stop." You must both clearly agree as to when you will commit to reengaging in the discussion once emotions have settled. It needs to be a bal-**

ance between the time one needs to get his body calm again (it could be as much as a day or two) and the other's need to know this will be discussed again reasonably soon. Respect for both people's needs is essential for this to work.

CHAPTER 2

Even in the Hardest Times, Divorce Is Not Inevitable

Norma, The Couples Therapist

She drove blue through green, her navy Subaru slicing along the tree-lined streets toward her office. Norma loved the pastoral setting of her practice, just fifteen minutes from the city, yet with windows looking out on evergreens. She thought it important to provide a warm and comfortable environment for her clients. The couch her couples occupied during sessions had been selected after hours of online searching. Her desk was spare, absent of pictures of her husband or three children. A mentor had told her long-ago that photos would lead to unwarranted and complicated comparisons from clients and could impede the therapeutic process. Indeed, her entire twenty-year professional career up to this point was a constant balancing act between creating a warm and relaxed, a human and humane, space for clients, while still maintaining a clear professional boundary. She had long-ago surrendered to the reality that the therapeutic relationship was a unique animal, encouraging both intimacy and distance simultaneously. Therapists wanted people to be able to eventually share their deepest fears, fantasies, and shame, but at the same time they had to look at clients and say, "Our time is up."

Norma had studied individual, group, family, and couples therapy. When she first registered to be part of the online *goodtherapy.org* website that prospective clients would use to search for therapists, she saw a collection of more than fifty different choices for practice concentrations. She could checkmark any or all of them, and initially she had projected the gamut, from "trauma therapy" to "substance abuse" and "relationship issues." Eventually, she pared it down to a handful of approaches. She kept couples therapy listed, despite the fact that she really didn't like working with couples. Everybody said they worked with couples. She wasn't about to abandon this source of clients and income. She was an experienced therapist and had worked with more than a hundred couples over the years.

Still, she felt that tiny bit of dread in the pit of her stomach when a couple was sitting in her waiting room. The strategies that seemed to work well with her individual clients were less effective with couples—because couples were just so difficult…with each other and with her. A suggestion for behavior change to an individual could be coaxed along, refined, and the results processed in the slower, more manageable individual therapeutic space. But, goodness, with couples, the atmosphere became emotionally volatile at breakneck speed. Norma felt like most of her energy went into simply controlling the session. Even in the most successful meetings, when she'd suggest tried-and-true rules for couples communication, her clients would genuinely thank her and then go home to abandon these rules at the first spark of conflict. She would sometimes look at her most obdurate couples as being immature or as examples of the infamous (among therapists) "coupling of the borderline personality with the narcissistic personality." When she'd try to help Bill understand Joan's reasonable request for help around the house, he'd act like Norma was on Joan's side and get defensive. When she'd explain to Joan how her critical anger only made Bill more defensive, Joan would act like Norma was on Bill's side and then withdraw for the rest of the session. Norma found that her most successful sessions occurred when she would do individual work with one partner in the presence of the other. She often heard the statement (from couples who had been together twenty years or more), "I never knew that about you!" Still, for all of her experience, skill, and intuitive gifts, Norma felt out of her depth when she faced a couple in conflict. She started to research the most successful and popular approaches to couples therapy. Her discoveries fascinated and absorbed her. For a month, her husband would have to drag her away from the computer to bed. There was The Gottman Method. There was Harville Hendrix's Imago Therapy. David Schnarch's Crucible Therapy concentrated on the couple's sexual connection. There were Ellyn Bader, Brent Atkinson, Stan Tatkin, Esther Perel, Terry Real and more, all of whom had their own take on working with couples. The list was far longer than Norma would have thought, the choices daunting. Then a close friend and colleague told her about an upcoming externship in an approach called Emotionally Focused Couples Therapy. She had heard its founder, Sue Johnson, speak at a conference the previous year and had liked her. Intrigued, Norma decided to register despite the cost and the four days of lost income it would entail.

THE CHALLENGE AND PROMISE OF COUPLES THERAPY

Regardless of age, sexual orientation, or length of time together, people enter couples therapists' offices everywhere with the same array of distressing complaints. Some of the most common reasons a relationship seems doomed would make any divorce naysayer come up short:

- The trust is gone.
- There has been too much damage after years of fighting and the things my partner has said and done.
- We are incompatible.
- We have grown apart.
- I don't love my partner the way I want or need to in order to stay married.
- I love my partner, but I'm not *in love with* him/her.
- My partner is a narcissist.

- My partner is mentally ill.
- We haven't had sex for ten years.

This certainly is a dispiriting list. I have often said in my office that, if left to their own devices, couples in high levels of distress won't manage to stay together. *Just staying together, though, is not the goal.* People mistakenly believe that the best they can do is to learn how to hold their noses and suffer through years of honoring their marriage vows. Usually, that becomes intolerable, and the people fly apart. The goal is not to find a way to *tolerate* each other—with staying together becoming a form of tragedy and emotional torture. The goal is to fashion a new, stronger, and sustainable bond. It can be done, and has been done, many thousands of times every year in all corners of the country. This chapter introduces you to the people who can join you in the work of healing a deeply wounded bond, how they think, and how they work. Let us first, however, address the threshold problem facing couples before they even make that first call to the therapist.

OVERCOMING THE
"WE CAN DO IT OURSELVES"
SYNDROME

In American culture, self-reliance and independence are bred in the bone. The very idea of turning to another person for help when our relationship is in trouble feels like an admission of weakness and failure. It is also a highly risky move, as we open the most private corners of our lives to a stranger. Such exposure is deeply unsettling—not to mention the possibility that this professional may confirm our partner's complaints about us. University of Washington's Neil Jacobson, a leading authority on couples therapy, noted some years ago that only 1% of divorcing spouses sought the help of a couples therapist in the year of the divorce. As mentioned earlier, his colleague, John Gottman, found that, on average, couples first sought the help of a relationship therapist six years after serious problems arose between them.

So, the first shift in perspective is to see the couples therapist as a professional who has chosen to make the study of intimate relationships their area of expertise. Judgment of one of the partners makes about as much sense as an oncologist telling the cancer patient that their malady is their own fault or the lawyer making a client feel ashamed because they got themselves into whatever legal fix brings them into the office.

All good couples therapists will have a *theory* about how intimate relationships go awry and the steps needed to quell the conflict and heal the rift that has been created. Empathy is a necessary, but not sufficient, quality for any therapist. They've also got to have an understanding of what's going on in front of them *and* to communicate that understanding to flustered, frightened and often furious people. This is, after all, their field of expertise.

Another point to bear in mind is that effective couples therapy is seldom going to be a quick fix. Successful couples therapy with partners who are in a lot of distress will take a minimum of four months of weekly meetings and the vast majority will require a longer term. Nine months to a year, or more, is not extraordinary. However long the course of treatment, it is important that this never be correlated in the people's minds with failure or terrible, horrible, extreme dysfunction. There are so many factors that can contribute to any couple's distress, that judgments about length of time in therapy are neither accurate nor helpful. This is not to suggest that an agreement on a goal, with a commensurate understanding of where you are, at any particular time, in the journey toward that goal isn't a critical element of your work together. Couples therapy is most assuredly *not* a process where struggling partners go to fight once each week for weeks and weeks on end.

Speaking of "once each week" it is important to commit to meeting with a degree of frequency. Every other week or longer is a recipe for costly frustration. As will be described in more detail later in this chapter, effective change in couples work requires each person to shift the perspective they have brought with them to the first session. I can almost *guarantee* that the couples therapist who will work best for you will have a different understanding than you do of what is going on when you fight and how you can proceed through the maze of your quarrels to achieve reconnection. If people allow more than a week to pass between each session, then usually the interim period will see each person lose focus on the healing perspective which was shared by the therapist. They will slide back to their prior thinking, which is laden with blame and defensiveness. Each session will then be an effort to regain traction and you will be doing this over and over and over again in each every-other-week meeting. The work will take longer and the chances of success will diminish. The whole process will feel like a dispiriting waste of time *and* money.

As with most everything, there are tried and true ways to do something that *work* and those that don't succeed so much. When considering how couples therapy *ought* to work, we should bear Einstein's adage in mind. You can't solve the problem of intimate conflict and alienation with the same thinking that caused it in the first place. This problem thinking is what makes many therapists, and their work with couples, vastly, and painfully, unsuccessful. Let's take a moment, first, to understand this threshold problem.

WHY COUPLES THERAPY
IS THE LEAST SUCCESSFUL KIND OF THERAPY

It might come as little surprise to those who have been disappointed in their couples therapy that this form of help is broadly unavailing. Research has confirmed this fact. The reason, at least to me, is obvious. Too many people who perform couples therapy shouldn't.

There are tens of thousands of excellent individual therapists out there. These are people who are well educated, conscientious, and quite effective. They sit with clients one-on-one and use whatever approach they have mastered to help people understand their lives through a different lens. Yet, when they work with a couple, they still think *individually*, and their effectiveness is sorely diminished.

As aptly noted on the website of the National Registry of Marriage Friendly Therapists:

> *Many therapists have never taken a single course in marriage therapy and have little or no supervised clinical training in this form of therapy. Most academic programs in psychology, psychiatry, social work, and counseling do not require a single course in marriage and couples therapy. Even when such a course is offered, it's an elective. Only therapists trained specifically in the profession of marriage*

and family therapy have required coursework in marriage therapy, but they may not have significant clinical training specifically with couples—just with "family units" of some kind. When therapists go into their clinical practice, they often drift into seeing couples because there is such a demand for this work. (A national survey of private practice therapists found that 80% do marriage therapy.) But this is a difficult, specialized form of therapy that should not be done without supervised training. The result often is poor therapy for which couples often blame themselves rather than the therapist. Couples are playing Russian roulette with their marriages when they pick up the phone book and call a random therapist.

For starters, when people sit down for the first time for couples counseling, almost invariably, *both* people feel blamed. Each person thinks, "If only the therapist can help me get him/her to *understand!*" Each might also fear that the therapist "won't understand me, and will also side with my spouse." People who are trained to do *individual* therapy and then practice couples therapy are always at some risk to become overly involved with what the people are arguing about. Whenever the therapist feels like an umpire, she will get lost. Every time the therapist says to herself, "I understand why he would be upset, but I can't quite understand why she should be upset—she doesn't sound so reasonable to me," she will get lost. These are all impulses of the individually trained therapist. This kind of thinking is a major reason couples therapy fails.

Another reason couples therapy fails is that the therapist does not know how to take control of a session, and the couple gets embroiled in one of their typical arguments. They leave the office dispirited and wondering what the point is. After all, they can have the same exact argument at home. Every time you are having the same frustrating argument in a therapist's office and you feel yourself getting tense and escalated and you just keep arguing, know that this shouldn't be happening. You *can* have this same argument at home. Why pay someone money to have that same endlessly frustrating argument in front of them? (Note that I say "endlessly" here. If people escalate to the point of frustration in a therapist's office, that won't be helpful. However, a good, living, example of a couple's style of interaction and conflict is vital information for the professional. So, some conflict should be expected—but the therapist must have control of the session and keep the heat at a manageable level.)

Another thing to beware is the couples therapist who tends to avoid seeing the couple together *as a couple*. When the pain and fractured energy in the room seem overwhelming, many therapists will separate the individuals and work with them one-on-one. While there are some excellent therapists who believe you can work on the relationship if only one person comes in to therapy, that's different from not seeing a couple together when they are both willing to show up. I have known many therapists over the years who work with couples, but who really don't like that mode. They might say, "I don't like watching them argue." Bill Doherty, one of the deans of the American couples therapy community, once watched and commented on a video recording of a fairly experienced therapist who pronounced to the couple that he had to terminate his work with them because it wasn't "safe" in the room. Doherty found nothing that would suggest that either partner was unsafe to the other. What the therapist was saying was that it was unsafe for *him* in the room.

Therapists (as well as solid, experienced mediators, as I discussed in the first book in this pair, *Divorce*) are comfortable working in the face of overt conflict. It is our job to keep the room safe for each person even when (*particularly when)* there is a lot of emotion and intensity in the room. I have told couples that I will not allow them to escalate, and I will stop them before their cycle starts spinning too fast, even if it means I have to get up and stand between them. I've actually done that a handful of times—but that's what you've got to do so that both people are completely confident that a different, and safe, space is created, which will not be overwhelmed by their jagged pain and heat. (My clients sit in two swivel chairs. It would probably be harder to stand between them if they sat on a couch—but some therapists are more nimble than I am.)

Another threat to healing intimate conflict is a person's individual therapist. When I go in to see my individual therapist, I want him to understand me and show compassion. This is the place many of us go to offload all the frustration, anger, and pain that accompanies grinding intimate conflict. That individual counselor has to be careful, though, not to jump on a bandwagon of "Ain't he (or she) a bum." With a handful of exceptions (domestic violence chief among them), there are always three stories when a couple is in conflict—each person's story and the combination of those stories—which lend the clearest picture of what is going on. If an individual counselor reinforces one person's story of a conflict and helps them feel like a victim of the other, that person is poisoning the relationship. Compassion and balance are essential in helping an individual locked in intimate conflict that threatens to blow the connection apart.

There are, disturbingly, therapists who see couples embroiled in chronic conflict (and it doesn't even have to be intense and volatile), and they suggest divorce (which is considered unethical by the American Association of Marriage and Family Therapists). This should never be suggested or encouraged by a couples therapist. Now, to be sure, if one or both people in a couple choose to end the relationship, it is not a failure of couples therapy. The goal is to heal the wounds that can be healed and to help people understand that what they think is an inevitable divorce (because of "X" event or factor) might not be so inevitable. While avoidable divorce can hopefully be avoided, many couples will emerge from good couples therapy and divorce. This is not a failure of couples therapy if the individuals have come away understanding the process that brought them to this point, and the work has helped them end in a humane way.

So, bearing in mind Einstein's brilliant observation that "we cannot solve our problems with the same thinking we used when we created them," let's consider the hallmarks of that changed perspective, shared by experienced, effective couples therapists:

- *Systems Thinking*: This means looking at the couple *as an entity unto itself* and not two individuals who are fighting. People act in specific, and often predictable, ways when they are in a relationship, and we *must* understand that particular dynamic and how it operates, in order to help the individuals caught up in relational conflict.

- ***Adult Attachment***: This is the force that drives the intensity of intimate conflict. When people say to their partners, "I don't have these fights with anybody else," or, "I don't feel this horrible with anybody else," it is because the intimate, bonded relationship is unlike any other adult relationship. It is our *adult attachment relationship.*

- ***The Role of Emotion***: Many is the poor soul hooked into intimate conflict who wishes with all of their being that the discussion could just be rational. That is impossible, though, because intimate relationships—particularly intimate conflict—are *all about emotion.* Emotion is not something to be feared or avoided, though, since it is at the heart of what pains us *and* how we resolve our conflicts.

- ***The Escalating Cycle***: When we are in high conflict with our partner, we get so wrapped up in what we are fighting about that we completely lose sight of the reality that we are being swept up *together* in a cycle of reaction and fear that can be self-perpetuating. The cycle hides in plain sight, so, if we can manage to shift our perspective, it will be exposed and we can manage our conflicts, come to resolution, and not feel personally assaulted during these times of high stress and pain.

- ***External Stressors:*** None of us is hermetically sealed. Our world impacts us. In fact, one sign of robust mental health is that we leave ourselves open to the world, allowing our lives to impact us and having the resilience to not be overwhelmed. Sometimes those external stressors are like additional logs that get heaped on a flame of our discord. We need to know this and be sensitive to the daily context of our lives.

Let's take a deeper look at each of these.

YOU CAN'T UNDERSTAND COUPLES
IF YOU DON'T UNDERSTAND "SYSTEMS"

Couples therapists (and divorce lawyers, too, for that matter), need to be trained in *systems thinking.* If a couple in conflict can begin to think of themselves as a system, in which each part (i.e. the person) reacts automatically to the other, they will be a long way toward calming their anxiety, anger, and pain.

Systems thinking is definitely not the way we normally understand ourselves in a relationship. Imagine a midday Manhattan intersection. Speed up the scene (a la time lapse photography): flows of pedestrians move to the corner, stop, and then stream across the street. Taxis make turns where there are spaces. It's like a circulatory system consisting of human beings. Maybe that young man is on his way to a job interview; the woman in her forties is a block away from her office, where she gives investment advice; there's the pediatrician, the college student, the mom anxious to meet friends for lunch, the junkie looking to score soon. Every individual person has their story and the story might be why they are at that intersection at that moment. Yet, their individual stories have little to do with how they move with the flow of other people. They stop on red and go on green. They avoid aggressive cab drivers forcing a turn. If it starts raining, they will either open an umbrella, hunch deeper into their coats, or disperse, seeking shelter. If one person trips and falls, the flow of pedestrian traffic will part around them. If they need help, somebody will give them a hand, and the space in the flow will close up again. While each person in this river of humanity has a compelling personal story, they are now simply a part of the city's flow. For the civil engineer trying to ensure that people get from here to there in a safe and efficient manner, it doesn't matter what makes up each person's fears and dreams. This flow of pedestrian traffic is seen by them, by necessity, as a system.

Our bodies are composed of billions of individual cells, each one of which operates in a complex manner. You don't think of your lover as a collection of cells, though. You see them (and react to them) as an entity composed of those cells, yet having an existence wholly separate from them. Our bodies are a biological system.

We are individuals, but we are also part of systems of which we are only a component part. As that part, we will usually act in predictable and repeated ways. As we do that, the greater system is operating in a consistent manner. Our families are systems. Our intimate relationships are *definitely* systems. All operate based on long recognized rules. It is how *you* act in a system. It is how *I* act in a system.

Here are some of the most important parts of systems thinking when trying to understand people in intimate relationships and how they get stuck:

Circular Causality: We are used to thinking in a logical way about causation. "I am pissed off at my wife because she gets furious at me for the smallest things. There might be something wrong with her, I don't know. I think she might have an anger problem or needs to go on meds." "I can't stand the way my husband talks down to me. It seems like whenever we have a disagreement, he is so condescending. If he doesn't respect me, I don't know why I should stay in this marriage." Find me a couple that is battling, and I guarantee you each person will have their *very good* reasons for hurt, withdrawal, or irritation.

One person is not holding up their end of the marital bargain about doing chores, or they are not looking hard enough for work, or they are depressed and not doing anything about it, or they are embarrassingly flirtatious, or they spend too much. It sounds straightforward, but that's just not how intimate conflict operates. To understand this is the first step to finding a healing solution.

Here's the key: Causation is almost always "circular," meaning, "I did this because you did that, and you did that because I did this." Looking for where it started, or who is ultimately to blame, is futile...and alienating. A classic example is a fight that sounds something like this:

Mona: "You are never home. I feel like I'm living alone, and if I wanted to live alone, I wouldn't have gotten married. I'm lonelier now than if I were alone. You stay after work with your friends and often aren't home in time to have dinner with me and the kids. You say you work late, but you and I both know that you hang out with people from work for at least a couple of hours a few times a week. I'm sick of asking."

Bert: "Well, I do work late and the beer after work is not only a way of unwinding, but it's also a way to continue talking about strategy in a more relaxed setting. I've told you for a long time that I might not be home for dinner during the week and I don't understand why you keep nagging me about it. To be honest, I avoid coming home because you just keep nagging and you're angry all the time. Who'd want to be around that?"

Mona (getting more annoyed): "Well, I resent your saying I 'nag' you, but, sure, I keep mentioning it because *you are never home*. If you came home to be with us more I'd sure 'nag' you a lot less."

Bert (a look of dismissal on his face): "Well, if you didn't nag me so much, I'd be home more often."

Mona: "If you were home more often, I wouldn't nag you so much."

Who's right? *They both are.* The problem they get stuck in is trying to figure out which one is "righter" by tracing the argument back to its start. Who is the original aggrieved party? Well, good luck doing that! The day I hear people agree about where these circular arguments started is the day I will run to a casino and put it all on black 24.

We *react* in our intimate arguments. I definitely do certain things in reaction to my partner doing something of her own, and she is just the same. Once you *get* the idea of circular causality, you can start to understand your relationship as an entity in itself. It looks like this:

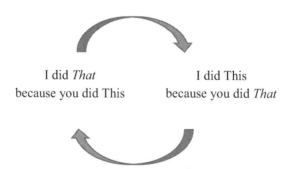

I did *That*   I did This
because you did This   because you did *That*

You will keep spinning faster and faster, and the arrows will become a wide circle.

People in intimate relationships play complementary roles: We are initially attracted to qualities in another person that we feel we lack—and vice versa. At the start (in the words of master therapists Kate Scharff and Lisa Herrick), we fit together like a "lock and key."[5]

Let's take a common pattern of the outgoing extravert and the withdrawn introvert.

Betsy grew up in a four-child family, and there was always something going on. The siblings all got along, for the most part, and dinners were noisy affairs in which everybody vied for the floor. All souls got attention, and Betsy was probably the most quick and verbal person in the family. She was always a bit of a whirlwind of energy. Throughout high school she was a joiner and always seemed to be busy. She has been a sales manager, with years of accolades for high performance to her credit. Louis is much more contained. As a kid, he loved to read and spent many happy hours alone with his books and, later, his guitar. He has a small number of close friends. When he and Betsy met, he was working as a software engineer.

In the beginning, Betsy was attracted to Louis's steadiness and reliability. She would often tell him he was her "rock." She loved their times alone at home when he would cook a great meal. Louis was drawn to Betsy's vivacity. She made life more fun and interesting, and together they'd do things he wouldn't dream of doing if he were on his own. She threw a surprise birthday party for him when he was thirty-five that people talked about for months afterward. This complementary fit wasn't so salutary as the years passed, but that is a story for a later section.

Another common pairing is the high-functioning person and the partner who tends to struggle. Dawn was the firstborn of three children. She felt a sense of responsibility from an early age and worked hard in school, where she was rewarded with excellent grades and glowing reports from her teachers. Both of her parents worked, and she received lots of affirmation for the way she took care of her two brothers and sister. She was a planner. In college, friends would come to her with their problems, and she gained a reputation of the shoulder others could cry on. By the time she met Brad, she was one of the youngest managers her bank had ever elevated to that level. Brad had been a playful and delightful child. The apple of his parents' eye, he was the middle of three kids. His asthma had been a problem when he was young and kept him from certain activities. Not a particularly diligent student, he got by on his good humor and winning way with others. He found college boring, and when he had the opportunity to work year round in Aspen, Colorado, he left at age nineteen to live a carefree ski bum life for a couple of years. At the urging of his father, he returned home and found a job in a real estate sales office. When he met Dawn, he was living in a two-bedroom, man-cave condo, bringing down six figures in a hot real estate market. She loved his spark. He loved the fact that she was a gourmet chef and made a beautiful home. When the market slumped, he lost his job. He told Dawn he didn't want to work anywhere that wasn't a challenge. She adored the playfulness he brought to her life and agreed to let him figure out his next move without pressure. Over the ensuing years, he worked in sales for various businesses, leaving after a year or three with complaints about management or compensation. He liked to spend, and Dawn put him on a budget. That worked for a few years.

Eventually, the gratification Dawn got from being needed by a boyish, charismatic guy began to shift to irritation and feelings of being taken for granted. Brad began to chafe at Dawn's "controlling personality." This symbiotic relationship, which had worked for each partner, began to sour as they both felt stuck in rigid roles. While Dawn and Brad came to resent the other, the painful reality is that each encouraged the other to take on their role and stick with it. Dawn was there to catch Brad when he fell. Truth be told, she loved to catch him. Helping others was always what she did well. It made her feel good about herself. Brad felt that he couldn't be truly alive without the flexibility that Dawn's groundedness allowed him. He compensated for not taking care of business by being romantic and playful.

There are many different varieties of fit that turn into twenty-ton weights as time passes and roles rigidify. The miser and the spendthrift; the emotionally expressive person and the quieter, more pensive partner; the person who is close to her family and the partner who is cut off from his. In each of these examples, and many others, there *is a good reason* that each person is drawn to the other. One important key to a long-term, comfortable, safe, supportive bond is moving to the point of saying, "That's my Steven," whenever he does his *thing* and yet still feels loved and accepted. Plus, he will be far more relaxed and kind when Sally's foibles arise. In a way, more than the excitement of passion and being "in love," it's the abiding knowledge that we are loved and accepted that allows us to pursue our own lives—you know, the one we started when we emerged from the womb alone and the one we'll end all on our own, too.

Couples have their own built-in emotional thermostat*:* Systems tend to resist change. While each individual might complain about the other and the relationship, they will both make constant little recalibration moves to keep the pattern of interaction from changing. That idea of an emotional thermostat is called "homeostasis." Any parent who has had a grown child living at home and unable to find work might understand this concept viscerally. Every time you worry about what will happen to him if he is forced to live on his own and, thus, avoid asking him to find a way of fending for himself, that's homeostasis at work. Every time he messes up and causes you to worry, that's homeostasis at work. It all keeps the status quo in order, and he remains at home.

One of the seemingly magical properties of systems and the nature of homeostasis is that at first (and maybe for a while) the system will resist any effort to change the way it operates—the fit and function of the various parts. If the stay-at-home spouse decides to look for work, that might cause her partner to become edgy and emotionally withdrawn. If the other spouse who works a hard schedule decides to cut back a bit to spend more time with the children, his partner might start commenting more insistently about the lack of available funds. If the submissive spouse becomes more assertive, this might cause his partner to become angrier than usual. Whatever the "fit" of any particular couple, if one finds the deadlock stifling and unsatisfying, and seeks to change the dynamic in some manner, that person will almost certainly meet some resistance from the other. If one seeks to change within the dynamic of an entire family system, the resistance is multiplied by the number of people in that system. People generally don't like discomfort and conflict and want to avoid it. Thus, an errant part of the system is drawn back into prior functioning...usually.

Yet here's the magic. Usually, if the person seeking to change hangs in there in the face of resistance, eventually the members of that system will adjust to accommodate the change, and the *entire system will change*. (Of course, some systems are pretty rigid and will resist change intensely. This could threaten the entire system, itself. If the submissive partner holds on to his new assertive stance, it might threaten to rupture the relationship. This is a time to get the support, education, and guidance of a professional who can point out the dynamics and give the couple the insight and strength to make the adjustments necessary to renew the relationship on a repaired foundation.)

Each couple has their own dance and the steps are well synchronized: A few years ago, Al Pacino won an Oscar for his role as a blind ex-military officer. In one stunning scene, he takes a young, beautiful woman in his arms and performs a seamless tango with her. That scene is an apt metaphor describing the dance almost every couple performs.

The most common step is the "pursuer/distancer." In most intimate relationships there is one partner who tends to pursue the other for connection. This connection can be long talks or expressions of feelings—or it can simply be time together. In any event, whether soft or sharp, these efforts at connection are often met by someone who tends to push for emotional space. These folks need some distance in order to breathe. That's in their nature. So what happens all too frequently is this dance, in which one person approaches the other and the partner withdraws. This might happen a few times, and then the pursuing partner will become hurt by what feels like rejection. She will close down in some way. He'll ask the inevitable, "What's wrong?" The response will often be, "Nothing," but the simple act of asking is the connection the pursuer is seeking, and she'll relax until the next time she feels too much of a space between them, and the dance will start over again. The pursuer/distance dance is central to our understanding of the most common pattern of intimate conflict and will be explored more deeply in a later section.

Beware the Emotional Triangle: What happens when you are annoyed or hurt by another person? Do you sit down with them and talk out your issue with them? If so, well, kudos to you! You are in a distinct minority in this human realm. Most people will find it difficult to confront the other with our complaint, not having had the benefit of a good manual like Stone, Patton, and Heen's *Difficult Conversations*. So, what do we normally do? We talk to someone else about our beef.

Bill and Martin just celebrated their second anniversary. Bill, who is the more romantic of the two, bought Marty, who is quite the clotheshorse, a pair of beautiful and expensive ties. He spent a long time thinking about what he wanted to say in the card he would give his partner. On their anniversary, Bill came home excited to share this special time with Marty and got a call telling him that Marty wouldn't be home until late because he had a project that needed completing at work. Bill was extremely put-out, but kept it to himself because he didn't want to rock the boat.

The next day, over lunch, he shared his let-down with Carla, one of his close friends. "I just can't believe Marty cares so little about all we've been through and how far we've come," moaned Bill.

"You know, Bill," piped Carla, "I've known Marty as long as I've known you and you have always been, *by far*, the most thoughtful one. I think it's a real shame how he treats you sometimes."

Hearing this, Bill's feelings toward Marty softened, thinking "He's not so bad, really." Meanwhile, Carla took a step away from Marty, checking up on him less and only texting him in response to pings from that direction. Things simmered down quickly for Bill, but it took a couple of months before Carla and Marty got back on track.

This is the emotional triangle at work. Stress or anxiety enters the relationship between Bill and Marty. Rather than address Marty directly, Bill siphons off his distress by complaining to Carla. Once he has done that, Carla has the choice to become triangled into the conflict or refraining. The moment Carla, the third person in the dynamic, sympathizes with Bill and *takes his side*, she has become triangled in. The dissonant energy between Bill and Marty *shifts* to the relationship between Carla and Marty and the waters between the first pair tend to calm. The only problem is that the issue that upset Bill in the first place is never addressed and will continue to fester. For now Bill is feeling okay, but he'll always remember this anniversary affront as an example of Marty's self-involvement and resent his relative lack of importance. One day a less dramatic disappointment may lance Bill's boil of hurt and resentment and Marty will be flabbergasted (and angry) over the intensity of the personal attack leveled at him.

The two-person relationship is considered by experts like Murray Bowen to be basically unstable. We cannot *always* get along without conflict and anxiety with the individual we are close to and when that anxiety starts to rise, like a growing electrical vibration, we will naturally seek to lower our discomfort by triangling in a third person. If that third person gently but firmly declines the invitation and insists that we talk to the object of our distress, the emotional triangle will not form.

Anyone, or anything, can be triangled in and if the conflict is intense enough (fueled, for example, by mental illness or emotional/physical abuse) one triangle will not be enough to contain the anxiety threatening to explode in this two-person system. Like the surface of a winter's pond, in which the crystalizing ice spreads, one couple can triangle in a child, their parents, the social service system, the criminal justice system and friendship network. Just as a pond's surface thickens during Winter's progress, the triangles can lock into place, freezing the original two people in a stalemate of unstated injuries and resulting chronic anxiety. To repeat a vital point made earlier, if we allow ourselves to be seduced by the subject matter of the conflict and miss the process (here, triangulation) we'll never see the tools we need to ease the distress and revive the longed-for connection.

UNDERSTANDING "ANXIETY"

We hear the word "anxiety" a lot. To understand how it operates within a relationship system, let's not think of it as a hand-wringing weakness. Rather, let's understand anxiety as a universal form of basic, visceral discomfort or unease, which exists in us, all the way down to the cellular level.

Anxiety is a natural reaction to a potential threat. Whenever we experience discomfort or conflict with someone close to us, we will *always* experience anxiety. We might not have conventional "anxiety" symptoms like sweating, shaking, dry mouth, and difficulty thinking clearly (then again, we might), but we will not be at ease and completely comfortable in our own skin. Here's the thing about anxiety: it will almost always be accompanied by automatic reactivity to our partner.

Because anxiety is uncomfortable and our intimate partner can trigger it easily, we are always vulnerable to reacting emotionally. That's not "acting" emotionally, it is "**re**acting" emotionally. The more intense our anxiety, the less we are able to think through our actions and the more liable we are to automatic reactions. Murray Bowen, one of the true giants of family therapy said,

> *As anxiety increases, people experience a greater need for emotional contact and closeness and, in reaction to similar pressure from others, a greater need for distance and emotional insulation. The more people respond based on anxiety, the less tolerant they are of one another and the more they are irritated by differences. They are less able to permit each other to be what they are. Anxiety often increases feelings of being overloaded, overwhelmed, and isolated, feelings that are accompanied by the wish for someone to lean on, to be taken care of, to have responsibility lifted.*

For many of us, this need to lean on another is distasteful, and, as we shall see later, might often cause a good deal of inner confusion. The anxiety that drives us so insistently in intimate relationships is attachment anxiety. Now is a good time to take our first look at attachment and its hold on our hearts.

ATTACHMENT:
THE TIE THAT BINDS AND THE FEAR OF LOSS

Mary Ainsworth had been a brilliant student and was supremely resilient. Her husband was an academic, as was she, and since the times (1960s and '70s) dictated the wife's accommodation to the husband's career, when he moved to pursue his education or received faculty appointments, she found herself uprooted and settling down again and again. In the course of her travels, she was introduced to the work of John Bowlby. She began to devote her extremely keen mind to the relationship between mothers and their infants. A residency in Uganda gave Mary a fertile ground for her research. As she is quoted in Robert Karen's excellent *Becoming Attached*, Ainsworth began to see that the babies were not just passive repositories of a mother's attention. Indeed, she observed:

> *These were very active babies. They went after what they wanted. I began to see certain behaviors that indicated that the baby was becoming attached, and I was able to list them in chronological order of appearance. There was, for instance, the differential stopping of crying. The mother picked up the baby, the baby would stop crying, but if somebody else tried to pick him up at that point, he would continue to cry. Differential smiling. Differential vocalizations. I began to see different situations where attachment to the mother could be spotted; and you could differentiate an attachment figure from some other person, even a familiar person.*

Eventually, Mary and her husband ended up in Baltimore, and she commenced a study that would become one of the most influential in the history of psychological research.

In the first phase of this study, she gathered together twenty-six expectant families and, with the help of associates, did a *lot* of observation in the first year of the babies' lives. Her co-investigators would make eighteen home visits of four hours each over that time. They noted how quickly (or slowly) the mother came to the infant in response to his cries, the frequency and comfort of the mother's breast-feeding efforts, and how responsive (or attuned) to the baby's experience the moms were. There was a wide variation in responses. They noted, for example, that some parents ignored 96% of their baby's cries, while others ignored only 4%.

At the end of the first year, Ainsworth had the mothers and their babies come to her lab, a room with a toy-covered floor and chairs for the adults. First, the mother and baby were left in the room for a short while. The babies, as expected, would crawl over to play with the toys. Next, a stranger would walk into the room and sit beside Mom. The baby's response (usually negligible) would be observed. Then the mother would leave the room. The baby's reaction would then be noted, and again a short time later when Mom returned. Next, the

_____

stranger would slip out of the room, and then the mother would exit again, leaving the baby completely alone in the room. After a brief time observing the baby's reaction, the mother would return. The child's response when the mother exited, and then when she returned, were the key points of observation. Thus was created the Strange Situation study.

As you would imagine, not all babies behaved the same way. The great majority did cry piteously when their mothers left them alone, and they approached their mommies enthusiastically upon her return. They were able to be easily absorbed in playing with the toys at the beginning and later upon the mother's return. However, a significant minority of the babies became so absorbed in their play that when their mothers left the room, they hardly paid notice and, upon her return, they just continued to play. A smaller minority responded quite a bit more dramatically. These babies would tend to be preoccupied with Mom even when playing with the toys, as if wanting to be constantly reassured that she was there. Upon the mother's exit from the room, they reacted intensely, just as did the first, larger, group. However, upon her return, the mother was unable to calm the baby, who would either reject her or would alternate between leaning into her and then kicking away. When put back on the floor, the babies would have a difficult time becoming engaged again with the toys.

Ainsworth described the babies' responses in terms of the "security" of their attachment to their mothers. That great majority who were able to enjoy the play, displayed distress upon mother's leaving, and were later able to be soothed upon her return were seen as "securely attached."

The babies who enjoyed the play and were almost nonchalant with the exit and return of their mothers were "avoidantly attached." One interesting side note on these little ones is that some observers might say that they were the most secure, since they seemed quite composed during the experiment. However, studies of their physiological reactions at that time showed that their hearts were racing and they displayed all the *internal* signs of heightened distress. They just didn't show it.

The smaller percentage of babies, who were both dramatic in

their distress and rejecting of their mother's ministrations upon return were the "anxiously attached" children.

When the behavior in the lab was correlated to the interactions between the mother and baby in the first year of life, Ainsworth and her colleagues saw a connection. For the securely attached babies, their mothers were, for the most part, responsive to their needs and attuned to their moods. This describes about 65-70% of all the babies who have gone through this study (many thousands of babies have been "strange situationed" over the forty-plus years since the original Ainsworth study).

The avoidantly attached little ones generally had a common experience in their homes in which their calls for distress were either ignored or brought negative responses from their mothers. These babies had clearly learned that external expressions of distress and need for comfort would not bring their caregiver, so they had learned to make do without that kind of connection. This group made up about 20% of the babies.

The anxiously (or sometimes called "ambivalently") attached babies experienced inconsistent caregiving. Sometimes they were comforted, other times ignored, and at other times were met with anger at their need for connection and comfort. These children grew to be unsure about the trustworthiness of their mother's presence for them, and oftentimes they would ramp up their attachment cries to make sure that they were attended to. This group accounted for about 10% of the total.

A much smaller, and heartbreaking, group of these babies would react in truly bizarre fashion upon their mother's return. They would do things like run partway to mother and then stop and fall to the ground, or they would approach their mothers backwards. These were the children who displayed a "disorganized" attachment style. They had usually been subject to frightening behavior and abuse from their caregivers.

The work of Mary Ainsworth, and others like her over the years, has helped us understand that attachment, while a need that is universal, is not met with the same response among all caregivers. This will affect the comfort we have in expecting, and seeking, close, secure connection with important others throughout our lives. Literally, from the first time our mouths seek out the nipple, we are learning how key people in *our* world and *our* lives will respond to *our* need for connection, care, and comfort. Most of us will be lucky and the message imprinted on our tiny brains will be that love is available to us. It can be trusted. It will not be withheld or suddenly yanked away for seemingly no reason. Cries of need or fear would not be automatically accompanied by (and later associated with) pain. Now imagine how calming that is to our nervous systems. If we are blessed with a temperament that also permits us to *experience* that security, we are counted among the truly fortunate.

This basic need (shared among all mammals) does not always meet the comforting presence of a consistently nurturing caregiver. Some of us learn that the love, warmth, and responsiveness we urgently seek will not be ours. We cry and we are left alone. We reach out in need and we are punished for doing so. Yet, we are resilient little souls and we will turn somewhere for that comfort. If people won't give us that soothing, we will turn to things to fill that need. Knowing we can't receive what we need from our breathing caregivers, we abandon the search in that direction. These avoidantly attached babies don't lose their need for nurturing care; they have just concluded that they will not find it in human connection.

Some babies get that love, but intermittently. It's not the kind of consistent failure to have that need met which the avoidant babies experience. They'll get it...and then they won't. They don't know whether to trust it. Receiving inconsistent care is excruciating. You get the taste for that love. Just when you might have relaxed into receiving comfort, it is wrested away, or, worse, the baby receives an angry rebuke for his need for comforting. At least the avoidant babies have learned to grow a callus around their hearts so the withdrawal of care won't hurt so much. With these anxiously attached little ones, it's like a scab is torn away every time there is sweet care-giving followed by the acute pain of its withdrawal.

So that's a brief story about babies and early attachment. Does it end when we start school, or begin to grow hair under our armpits, or leave our family homes and enter the world of work and start our own families? Nope, it doesn't. And why would it? As Sue Johnson notes, "Dependency, which has been pathologized in our culture, is an innate part of being human rather than a childhood trait that we out-grow." This need for connection is hardwired into our brains. In fact, there have been many studies of the "adult attachment style" of thousands of people who were "strange situation" babies. Leading researchers have estimated that there is about an 80% or more correlation between early attachment and later attachment styles.[6] What do those later styles look like?

Before we get into this discussion, a word of caution is warranted. When it comes to understanding how people operate in the world after exposure to different stresses when they are young, we must always remember that we are on a continuum. People might demonstrate certain behaviors, and they might even be annoying behaviors, but we have to go quite a distance before we consider those behaviors an "impairment." For the most part, these adult attachment styles are tendencies in a particular direction and should not lead to an automatic assumption that there is something wrong with that person. It's just a way of being in the world, with its benefits and drawbacks.

So back to the discussion. The vast majority of people who tended to have a secure attachment as babies will grow into adults with a "secure" attachment style. Within a broad range, these people will be able to have intimate relationships of decent duration. These people do not have a constant anxiety about the risks posed by intimate bonds and feel basically confident that they can have a securely attached relationship with a partner, so the distress caused by intimate conflict is neither deep nor long.

Those babies who learned to soothe themselves, the "avoidant" children, will often grow up to have an adult "dismissive" attachment style. These people have learned from an early age that their world will not include the available other upon whom they can rely for emotional care. They learn to navigate through the world, getting their attachment needs met elsewhere—through work, sporting activities, acquisition of objects, and the like. They will usually get married and have children. Their partners might find them to be distant, but many couples develop excellent compensatory strategies and do just fine when one or both have a dismissive attachment style. Of course, the further along the continuum one finds himself, the deeper will be his partner's expressed distress about emotional distance—to the point that some people with a dismissive attachment style do just fine on their own.

The babies who were described as "anxiously" attached will likely grow into adults with a "preoccupied" attachment style. This term reflects these people's preoccupation with the safety and security of their intimate relationships. Their level of anxiety when confronted with a close bond, *especially* when it might become shaky for any reason, would be likely to rise. There is always hope (so deep, it's almost on a *cellular* level) that they can find that secure closeness with a significant other, coupled with intense fear (again on a *cellular* level of depth) that they will be disappointed. They might even have been caused to feel shame for their longing and expectation that such closeness can be achieved. Conflict will only push that anxiety to a higher level. Not knowing how to manage the combination of need, fear, disappointment, and shame, this person will often reach out to their partner in the only way that feels safe—with criticism, being sure to point out what he or she is <u>not</u> providing.

It is important, again, to remember that there is a "dismissive" flavor of people who approach one end of the "secure" range and there is a "preoccupied" flavor of people who approach the other end. Most of us will tend to either be reaching out for relationships or experiencing some hesitance about the complexities and intensity of intimate relationships. In fact, Murray Bowen believed that we *all* experience an inner tension between connectedness to another and autonomy. One need tends to be stronger in each of us.

However you might see yourself and your partner, one thing is very likely for you both: Each person is seeking, in their own way, a secure attachment with a significant other. As adults, this is the most important relationship in your life. Within this bond, we seek and receive physical closeness through touch (both affectionate and sexual); a safe haven, where we may turn when the world feels threatening; and a secure base, from which we may explore our world. When the security of this bond is threatened by conflict, anxiety floods our being. We feel it in the depths of our souls, and our reactions become automatic. Suddenly, we are launched into a dance that becomes self-perpetuating. It is often described by therapists who think in terms of attachment as a cycle. Like any cycle, while each person reacts to the other, all those frantic attempts to mark the start (usually at the feet of the other) will only frustrate and shove people farther apart.

ATTACHMENT-BASED THERAPIES

The idea of working with people from an attachment perspective has been around for a long time. Carl Rogers might be the most important psychologist of the twentieth century, post-Freud, yet (strangely) he is little known today among non-therapists. Raised in the rural Midwest, Rogers developed his independent thinking in this environment of devout, hardworking people. In the early 1940s, in a professional world that was dominated by Freudian analysis or life solutions prescribed by psychological "experts," Rogers was the first to say that emotional healing arises from the *relationship* between the two people sitting across from each other.

It was not a notion that was exactly *embraced* by the powers that be in the field, but the force of Rogers's thinking and the integrity of his personality forged the beginning of Humanistic Psychology. Today, almost everyone practicing counseling—regardless of their "theoretical approach"—is grounded in the work of Carl Rogers.

Think for a moment—what would you need at the most basic level in a relationship with a counselor, the person with whom you talk about sensitive and very private stuff?

First, there has to be a sense that the other person "gets" you and your life situation. The counselor needs to convey that you are truly seen. There needs to be a sense of resonance—the attunement that we ardently sought with our primary caregivers.

The second requirement is that this resonance must be accepting. We might have had plenty of unsatisfactory (or worse) experiences of being "gotten" by another person, but then judged, manipulated, or dismissed by them. So the message needs to be, "I understand, and you are accepted in my eyes."

The third element of this kind of relationship is that this "getting you" and "accepting you" message has to be conveyed in as trustworthy a way as possible. The experience of the counselor must be genuine, and *conveyed* as genuine. Some of us are used to getting positive messages that lay on top of falsehood.

Our antennae for untrustworthiness is super acute. The attachment needs of the baby are satisfied by honest and loving attunement. The same is true for us as adults.

Rogers understood this. He said that a truly healing counseling relationship consisted of the following three elements: (1) Accurate empathy, (2) Unconditional positive regard, and (3) Genuineness.

Rogers demonstrated that people are capable of finding their own answers within a relationship marked by these three factors. Similarly, Sue Johnson has often stated that couples who are in conflict over particular issues will be able to figure out their own solutions once their relationship returns to a caring balance, marked by the ability to shift from (natural) self-protection to empathic (and non-self-blaming) understanding of their partner's pain in the relationship, conveyed with love and nurturance and honesty.

In describing one of the pillars of Emotionally Focused Therapy, Johnson has said,

> *EFT is essentially a humanistic approach to therapy.... Humanistic therapists view people as primarily social beings who need to belong and feel valued by others and are best understood in the context of their relationship to others.... It is not surprising, then, that the acceptance and empathy of the therapist are considered to be a key factor....*

The acceptance of the therapist, or what Rogers termed "unconditional positive regard" for each client allows clients to encounter their experiences in new ways.

The enthralling process of couples therapy shifts from the care and understanding of each person's pain in the relationship, as reflected in the early exchanges between the counselor and each individual, to the ability of each partner, over time, to openly share their pain, fears, and dreams with the other—and be welcomed into the open arms of acceptance and care by their partner. People enter couples therapy almost certain this can never happen, and yet it is the explicit goal of attachment-based couples therapy, and it is achieved with many struggling couples.

COMMON FIGHTS
FROM AN ATTACHMENT PERSPECTIVE

Many kinds of arguments step into a couples therapist's office. They are content-rich and cry out for the referee to declare a winner and loser:

Jean does all the work around the house and resents it, while Bill can't count all the things he does without any acknowledgement from Jean—he just gets complaints.

Ron lost his job last year and it was a blow to his ego. He is making efforts to find work but it's hard. Elliott gets home from work at 5:30 and Ron is playing video games. Elliott is angry Ron is not doing more to find a job. Ron is angry because Elliott doesn't understand how hard it is out there.

Earl is an outgoing guy with a wide circle of friends and work colleagues, a number of them women. He likes keeping in contact with these people, but whenever he has lunch with one of his women friends, Roberta is furious. She doesn't understand why he *has* to have lunch with these women. He becomes angry in response. Roberta is invading his life and making business networking difficult for him.

Dwayne and Jill are excited when their first baby comes, but Jill becomes hypercritical of what seems to be Dwayne's lax attitude around care of the child. One afternoon, he leaves the baby alone on the living room floor for ten minutes while he cleans the kitchen, and Jill thinks it's the most thoughtless, dangerous thing she's ever heard anyone do. Dwayne becomes angry in return, telling her to calm down. *She's* not God's gift to parenthood, either!

As mentioned before, many therapists who are trained and think in terms of individuals will find themselves plopped in the middle of these continuous arguments and try to act like referees. When an issue triggers something from their own life, there is quite the risk that the therapist will find himself siding with one person. That is the quickest way to blow up a session and ruin a relationship with the couple. There is a far more helpful way to understand these kinds of fights and many others.

We all have emotional triggers. Someone close to us can say or do a particular thing, and our anger level goes from zero to sixty in a nanosecond. Those buttons are different for different people:

An intimation from Leslie that Norm is incompetent, because she suggested that maybe they should get her brother, Don the electrician, over to help install the lighting fixture, sends Norm stomping out of the room. That's a sensitive place for Norm, yet it might not be so for another person.

Lou forgets to bring the bouquet home from the office that he got for Jamie on their anniversary. Jamie is distraught and tells him not to bother driving the ten minutes back to the office to get the flowers. His apologies, beautiful card, and plans for a romantic dinner do nothing to change Jamie's mood. Another person might not have that particularly raw and painful button.

Buttons get pushed all the time in our intimate relationships. Sometimes we get triggered into a cycle that starts spinning around so fast, and so quickly, that people feel swept away by its rapidity and force. When I get emotionally charged about something and react strongly to what my partner has done, it is an excellent bet that she will react to my reaction and we will start spinning faster. What causes these automatic and intense reactions? We don't get anywhere by saying that it's obvious, that anybody would react that way: That's actually not true. Loads of people would not react so strongly (they react strongly to something else). What triggers your strong reaction is deep inside of you, and a big part is related to your attachment anxiety.

In the incredible work done by Dr. Sue Johnson and others, certain common themes have been identified, which are aroused when we experience attachment anxiety in conflict with our partner. With even the gentlest probe, these themes come spilling out in the consultation room. One person usually has a lot of emotional energy directed toward the relationship. The sense of disconnection from this one deeply important person can really spin their head around. "I feel unimportant to him." "I am invisible." "I am her fourth priority, if that." "I wanted a teammate, but instead I feel so alone."

While one person is often reaching for their partner, the other is just as frequently tentative about embracing that connection. Maybe they have a slightly avoidant attachment style and have found the peace of retreat to be their refuge. Very often, the frustration and anger expressed by the pursuing partner stings more than the withdrawing partner lets on; it might sting more than *they realize* at the time. I have heard many descriptions like "diving into a bunker" or "surrounding myself with a protective shell." The experience might be expressed a number of ways. "I don't think I'll ever be able to give her what she wants." "No matter what I do, it's never enough, so I feel like giving up." "I just go numb."

Thus begins the cycle that sweeps in and takes over the relationship with its independent force. The partner feeling alone will reach out intensely for the other, usually after years of feeling ignored, dismissed, or not taken seriously. The other will feel the heat of dissatisfaction and believe they are a disappointment. The part within that says, "You can fool most everyone but, really, you know that you're not good enough," increases its volume and intensity. It hurts like hell and he withdraws for safety. There are many possible avenues for withdrawal: He can get on the computer or start drinking or leave the house or overwork or just shut down emotionally. While there are many different styles of withdrawal, what they all have in common is that the person's partner feels even more alone, unheard, and abandoned. So she'll up the volume of her protests. The more intense she gets, the more he'll psychologically curl up into a ball. The more he shuts down and is inaccessible, the more distressed and angry she gets. Until the people get an idea that this is what is going on for them, they will be caught up in the swiftly spinning cycle—the faster it goes, like all centrifugal force, the more lovers are pushed away from each other.

THE PIVOTAL ROLE OF EMOTION

Emotions drive us. They can't be banned from our brain (as we will see later). A noted expert in the study of emotion, Paul Ekman, found that a handful of fundamental emotions were both universal (shared by cultures as different as indigenous people in New Guinea and suburbanites in the U.S.) *and* triggered similar facial expressions in widely different societies. These basic emotions included anger, sadness, fear, surprise, disgust, and joy.[7]

Emotion is also an essential force that drives decision-making. While many labor under the mistaken belief that logical decision-making is stripped of emotion, research neuroscientist Antonio Damasio demonstrated "Descartes' error" in his book of the same name.[8] He described a man who had a part of his brain, which held emotional reactions, removed due to a tumor. While the man remained pleasant, intelligent, and in almost all ways "normal," he became incapable of making any decisions. While he could accurately list the factors that would support each competing choice, he could not make these choices! He was incapable of holding a job, and his life seemed to disintegrate around him.

In like fashion, it is impossible to help intimate partners who are in distress without honoring the significance of emotion. Simple reliance on homework and attempts to train one partner to *act* differently, without the corresponding inclusion of emotions and their impact, will usually be doomed to failure.

When Sue Johnson first described a fairly focused *couples therapy* that was based on an understanding of adult attachment, she didn't call it *Attachment-Based Couples Therapy*. Instead, this approach was given the title *Emotionally Focused Couples Therapy*. As she has observed, "Emotions are privileged precisely because they orient people to their world and tell people what they need and fear."

The one compelling force that brings us together with an intimate partner and also can drive us away is emotion. It isn't reason or logic or common sense. I've experienced businessmen or women who come to couples therapy desperately seeking "tools." (This is particularly true for someone who has used an executive coach.) Such people are very results-oriented and want a plan. They are seeking a strategy to get the job of marital harmony accomplished. If only it could work that way! The world of intimate bonds is the world of emotions—a field of reactions and hidden desires for safety and acceptance that we all long for. All of us. Those who try to work on a strained relationship, and only want a recipe of things to say or do, will miss the key element of what makes these bonds intense, vital, and unique in our lives.

Our culture doesn't exalt emotion or emotional expression. I have laughed for years about the legal culture's disdain for anything "touchy-feely." Of course, a feeling that doesn't render us vulnerable, like anger in most cases, is a "feely" that is okay. Many of us don't possess a good "emotional vocabulary" and have a hard time recognizing our innate reactions to life's events when they come up. Lots of people have difficulty recognizing a feeling beyond "frustrated," which I have found to be a general, catchall term that can mean angry, frightened, embarrassed, worried, sad, or confused. For many in our culture, emotions are distractions, often beside the point and annoying. Strong emotions add unwanted drama to many life pursuits that require dispassionate focus. Work is an arena that doesn't welcome emotion, for good reason. Household tasks, sports activities, and meeting challenges of all kinds, generally don't go better with strong feelings. However, there is one area that is *almost all about emotions*.

You simply cannot evict emotions from your intimate personal relationship. That's a hard message for anyone who is uneasy about their emotional world. Many people simply don't know what's deep inside and feel frustrated and inadequate if asked to describe their emotional reactions. Others (*many* others) have had searing experiences when they have shared strong feelings. We are chastised in our youth for expressing strong emotions, particularly painful ones. I have known people who were raised by emotionally guarded parents who responded to "I'm mad" or "I'm sad" with, "No, you're not." Because emotions are so visceral (arising spontaneously and without a lot of thought or preparation), they can feel out of control and frightening.

We are human. Hard as we try, we all have places in our hearts where we experience fear and love and grief and embarrassment and longing. Life may render these emotions more intensely felt in some more than others, but we all have those spaces. We all can be hurt and we all do what seems right to not get hurt. Sometimes those strategies work. For many of us, that protection can be found in a tall, thick emotional wall that shields our hearts from others in our world. Yet the one place that will always touch the full range of our emotions will be our intimate personal relationship. To think about marriage (or marriage-like relationships) stripped of emotion is like a Van Gogh painting without color or a baseball game without a ball.

DEALING WITH HIGH EMOTION
~ THE ESCALATING CYCLE ~

The more Randy gets angry at Lou, the more Lou shuts down and backs off. The more Lou shuts down and backs off, the angrier Randy becomes. Gottman has observed that conflict isn't the problem in troubled relationships, reciprocal escalation of hostility is. People push each other to the next level and then the next level after that. We try again, again…and *again* to get through to the other person, and they always seem to react with defensiveness and anger rather than understanding and compassion. Many times I have heard, "I'm just saying how I feel, and she gets angry. It's just not safe." That makes us angry in return. If we can just see what we are doing as a process, rather than getting wrapped up in convincing the other person that we are right (or at least not crazy), we can slow things down and make contact. Sadly, and predictably, when people end up in a couples therapist's office, they've been escalating and firing each other up for a long time.

I have seen people in my office who seem as if their very survival is at stake when I experience the intensity of their anger at or judgment of the other. At the extremities of our distress and fear, we can say and do some horrible things to one another. These words or deeds cut deep. I have seen people who are good, kind, and brimming with integrity say incredible things to their partner that are only designed to wound—and wound, they do. The walls of every couples counselor's office have resonated with stories of hot words and devastating acts. Even though people might have shifted to an altered state and pushed each other to physiological overload, the felt transgressions are hard to forgive and harder to forget.

The pain at receiving this blow from our lover, our intimate partner, is sharp. This is because of the attachment bond that has been created and is now threatened. Let's go back to our initial needs to be seen, cared for, and protected in our early lives. Many of us (perhaps most of us) had these tender, vital, and consuming needs thwarted when we were young. This left many with a deep, yet not consciously recognized, sense of shame for our fundamental being (after all, this is what was rejected, when these needs were unfulfilled, or we were even punished). Perhaps you might not resonate with the word or notion of "shame" because it feels overly intense, but somewhere inside we carry some combination and gradation of feeling completely alone or inadequate or unlovable. We might silently despair of ever being with another person and being truly accepted—to find that safe harbor where we don't have to protect ourselves from buffeting winds of judgment or rejection *"if they really knew what was inside."* Most of us who carry these wounds learn to cope and carry on. We can be attractive, smart, sociable, supportive, accomplished, or supremely self-sufficient. Any one or a combination of these attributes—or any number of others—helps us get through life. Yet, there is a niggling voice, if we are attuned to it, that yearns for a safe place—"where I can be myself."

What often draws us into the intense bond of an adult intimate relationship is that the voice whispers to us (whether we *hear* it, the voice *registers*), "Here, you have found someone who *understands*." You intuitively sense that this person might have experienced loss, or fear, or shame in the recesses of their early life that somehow resonates with your own, and that they are a safe harbor. You never talk about it. You might not even realize it. Yet, if this is so, it certainly explains the intensity of the hurt, anger, and sense of betrayal when, in the throes of the inevitable intimate conflict, this person *flips* from uniquely safe, to dreadfully unsafe. To have taken the risk to open up, only to be judged and rejected (and even brutally attacked) is painfully destabilizing.

The first step toward re-stabilization is the understanding that a runaway emotional cycle is like a devil that seizes and contaminates an intimate bond—where so much is needed and at stake. With most of us, the damage inflicted is spawned by fear, not evil. That may help us back away from the abyss created by the harshness of the conflict. The better strategy is to recognize your cycle and learn how to slow it down rather than letting it feed off itself like a Midwestern tornado.

YOUR RELATIONSHIP IN CONTEXT
~ LIFE *DOES* HAPPEN ~

Every relationship has its own unique trajectory. A handful of people can claim this kind of story:

> *You have met your partner in your mid-twenties to early thirties when you were starting on our life paths. You were blessed to be extremely compatible and healthy. Your kid(s) came after a decent time with just the two of you alone to deepen your bond. You have never had serious financial stresses, and your relationships with your extended families are, for the most part, supportive and free of negative drama. You never struggled with addictions, depression, or other emotional challenges. Your kids all grew to be fine young men or women with a relative absence of frightening detours. No accidents, no illnesses, no crimes—just the normal challenges of getting from here (thirty) to there (ninety).*

Who can say this has been their fortunate lot? Certainly, just about no one who enters my office can claim a life free of crises. Many people were married in young adulthood, when they still were unsure of their feelings (not to mention their feelings for each other). Some have had a child already or one on the way. Depression has stolen the security of many relationships. Since 2008, if you have managed to dodge the hardships handed out by our shifting economy, you know you are among the truly fortunate. The deserts and killing fields of Iraq and Afghanistan have extinguished the peace in the hearts of tens of thousands. This is just a tiny sample of the stresses that make life challenging for the struggling couple.

Even the "normal" life transitions put a strain on marriages. Birth of the first child marks the decline of marital satisfaction for the overwhelming majority of couples. More women are working out of the home than ever before. A family with two working adults robs the couple of time to attend to their relationship. Fatigue, worry, and pre-occupation with external stressors dampens sexual interest. Reduced (or nearly absent) sexual intimacy erodes a large part of a couple's foundation. The arrival of a second child increases the attention to be devoted to parenting, and away from each other, by a factor much greater than twofold. Holidays bring a yearly juggling act between each person's family obligations. Aging parents draw added time and attention away from your relationship.

Just as we can understand the process of our emotional cycle as lying outside of the subject matter of our particular fight, we can understand the entity of our ongoing relationship as being challenged by life events. I mean, *no wonder* you think the other person isn't who you think you married during a time when you are struggling with a child's illness. Little surprise that you think your spouse is an unfeeling shrew because she doesn't get how hard it is for you to have been out of work for the last year. We have to look at these events and circumstances as being the petri dishes that support and impact our lives. Label your partner all you want during these times, you'll just be drifting further from the truth.

Life happens. It's going to put stress on your relationship. If we feel cracks beginning to form in our foundation, it's wise to get some help.

THE WEIGHT OF THE WORLD
~SPECIAL CHALLENGES~

Sometimes it's helpful to think of ourselves as a car traveling down a country road. You can be a Subaru Sedan, Chevy Suburban, or anything you please. There will be bumps and potholes in this country road and, if your shock absorbers are good, you'll get to your destination without incident. Think of your basic mental health as those shock absorbers. If you are struggling with a locked-in, rigid approach to handling your challenges, this is going to make your journey much more uncomfortable. In fact, the presence of a personality disorder or substance abuse problem or pattern of domestic abuse might weaken your psychological shock absorbers so much that the merest dip in the road will cause you to come crashing to earth (and, to extend the metaphor, blow out the oil pan underneath). *It is impossible for most of us to summon the resilience necessary to forge a safe, intimate connection with this weight on our shoulders.* This is *not* a discussion of blame. We must attend to our vulnerabilities during times of high stress. We all need support, especially when life is particularly confusing and threatening.

The extraordinary challenge of creating a safe connection from behind the walls of a locked-in personality disorder or untreated substance abuse or the cruel prison of domestic abuse applies with equal force to those facing divorce. The major difficulty in addressing these problems is that divorce *always* comes with blame. You will feel blamed by your spouse for conduct that led to the end of the marriage and bent into a defensive crouch to ward off attacks on your character. You will also blame yourself. In the context of divorce, you'll be so preoccupied with protecting yourself against these assaults, there will be little if any chance that you'll have the ability to recognize and deal with your loose shock absorbers. But deal with them you must. Let's look at each one of these psychic weights and how they complicate the road to reconnection.

Personality Disorders

The very sound of it is intimidating. Sounds like a big deal and, indeed, it can be. One of the best descriptions I have heard of personality disorders was in an article discussing why they are such a challenge in divorce:

Bill Eddy, an authority on "high conflict personalities" does a great job of describing the cycle of distress suffered by these unfortunate people and how they manage to push others away and bring heightened conflict into their lives. It goes like this:

These people experience chronic feelings of INTERNAL DISTRESS, although they…think the distress is EXTERNAL, so they…BEHAVE INAPPROPRIATELY to relieve the distress, but of course…the   DISTRESS   CONTINUES   unrelieved,   and they…RECEIVE NEGATIVE FEEDBACK, which heightens distress, which they think is external so they BEHAVE INAPPROPRIATELY…

Theodore Millon, a well-recognized expert on personality disorders and author of a major text on the subject,[9] described the challenges similarly:

> *Personality disorders tend to exhibit a tenuous stability, or lack of resilience, under conditions of stress. The coping strategies of most individuals are diverse and flexible. When one strategy or behavior isn't working, (non-personality disordered) persons shift to something else. Personality disorder subjects, however, tend to practice the same strategies over and over again with only minor variations. As a result, they always seem to make matters worse. Consequently, the level of stress keeps increasing, amplifying their vulnerability, creating crisis situations, and producing increasingly distorted perceptions of social reality.*

And so it goes, to the pain and consternation of all involved. And while these challenges can alienate others, it is important to understand that personality disorders are normal and adaptive behaviors, which have been pushed to an extreme.

There are a number of ideas put forth about the genesis of these psychological burdens. Some experts contend that they are part of a person's natural temperament, "hardwired" into their psyches. Others understand personality disorders as reactions to the behaviors of caretakers. How might the nurture-focused person understand the personality disorder?

There are those among us who experienced constant emotional difficulties in their families at an early age (before three). Because the assaults on their little psyches were so unrelenting, they had to develop a kind of psychological armor just to adapt to what was going on. Eddy thinks of personality disorders as reflecting adaptations to parental behaviors that were experienced by the child as repeated acts of abandonment or domination, or messages of basic inferiority, or the experience of being ignored. Personality disorders are about self-protection in the extreme, which becomes maladaptive behavior as we move into adolescence and, later, adulthood. While there are a number of different personality disorders that are recognized in the mental health world, only four are identified by Eddy as "high conflict personalities" and, therefore, are particularly challenging in divorce. These are the narcissistic, borderline, antisocial, and histrionic personalities.

To be in relation with the *narcissistic personality*, we experience this odd life orientation in which *only* that which is seen through *their* eyes is real or has value. It is their world, and the rest of us are all secondary bit players, there to ornament their inflated selves. Narcissists carry a sense of grandiosity that becomes unbearable for their relations, who constantly fight to be seen and heard. It has been said that the only way you get a narcissistic personality into therapy is when everybody in their life abandons them and they begin to experience a sense of depression for the first time in their adult lives. This person is extremely empathy-challenged, with an utter absence of the ability to appreciate another's experience. As with the antisocial personality, these people can be exploitive of others because of this lack of empathy.

When I think of the *borderline personality*, I envision a road stretching behind the person, strewn with the wreckage of shattered personal relationships. Borderlines (and whoever came up with that label for this personality should be embarrassed, as it doesn't describe anything and sounds too pejorative) suffer from a profound sense of inner emptiness. As a result, these people will tend to idolize another person in a relationship...that is, until the other person disappoints them, which is inevitable. When that occurs, the borderline personality often feels deeply betrayed, and the shame and anger that follows can feel like a nuclear blast. Borderlines I have encountered are frequently intelligent interpersonally and have an intuitive sense for others' emotional buttons. Thus, when they go on the attack, they draw blood. Borderlines are also characterized by impulsive and self-destructive behavior. You would be inclined to feel deep compassion for the inner pain carried by these people, if you didn't have to protect yourself from the injuries they often inflict.

The *antisocial personality* disorder is basically distinguished by a rejection of societal norms, a tendency to be a high-risk personality, a general absence of remorse for the negative impact of their behavior on others, and a tendency toward irritability, aggression, and deceitfulness. Bear in mind that this is at the extreme end of the spectrum for these kinds of traits. If your spouse lies and gets angry a lot, that definitely does *not* mean that they must have an antisocial personality. People who commit criminal acts characterize this personality style.

Finally, there is the *histrionic personality*. This person must be the center of attention, and drama is their constant companion. Their problems are *enormous*, their personalities *huge* and often flashy. Women laboring under the burden of this personality style can be quite overtly and unabashedly seductive.

It is also important to continually bear in mind that these represent extreme expressions on a continuum that passes through behavior that would be considered normal, and even socially laudable, and then moves into the opposite, and equally troubling, extreme.

For example, Millon notes that the overblown self-image of the Narcissistic Personality Disorder is an extreme variant of the person who has a healthy sense of self-esteem. If the pendulum were to swing to the opposite pole, we might see the person who feels themselves to be worthless and chronically depressed.[10] The Borderline Personality Disorder, marked by overwhelming emotional outbursts and movement toward merging psychologically with an idealized other, is an extreme position along a line that moves through a healthy expression of emotion and connection, to the opposite extreme of utter absence of emotion or desire to connect intimately with others. The Antisocial Personality Disorder swings from disdain for societal norms, through the appropriate openness to taking reasonable risks, and balancing personal values with societal needs, all the way to the extreme of paralysis over what others might think. The Histrionic Personality Disorder pendulum passes through a tolerance of attention by others through to the extreme of absolute withdrawal and feeling the attention of others is a crisis. Bear in mind that the range of "normal" is broad, and we must be careful not to dismiss another as "disordered" when they exhibit strong tendencies in a particular direction.

The key, again, is that each of these personality styles feels "locked in" and immune to environmental influence. Because these are fairly rigid systems of response, these people will often act quite inappropriately to environmental stimuli. While it is hard to feel compassion for these people if you have been cheated by the antisocial personality; dismissed and disdained by the narcissistic personality; burned by the borderline personality; or forced to indulge the histrionic personality, these unfortunate souls are clearly stuck in painful defense patterns that they learned at an early age.

Addiction and Substance Abuse

"I'm not an alcoholic," says she, as a full bottle of wine is consumed with seemingly little effect. "Nor am I," adds he, as he tries to remember what he did last night between sitting down in the booth over dinner and waking up this morning lying on his bed in his clothes. "Don't look at us," says the couple who share both hard alcohol before and wine with dinner every night. Those who live with alcoholics have heard every kind of denial there is. They can handle their booze. They can stop any time they like.

There are certain unalterable facts about alcohol abuse, besides the consistent presence of denial. It is a progressive disease because, as with all addictive substances, our bodies build a tolerance. There is a certain shame attached to admitting the addiction. There is a lot of deceit and hiding that accompanies the behavior. It almost always starts by helping us feel better and ends up making us feel far, far worse. Perhaps most importantly for our purposes here, it impairs clear thinking and sound decision-making.

Also, intimate conflict is escalated to frightening degrees by the inclusion of alcohol into a volatile mix. The reason is simple, inescapable, and quite biological. The front of our brains, right behind our foreheads, is the prefrontal cortex. It has a lot of functions, but one of the most important is that our mental brake pedals sit right there. Every time we have an emotional reaction and we want to say or do something rash, it's the prefrontal cortex that says, "Whoa there! Hold on a second. This is probably not a good idea." Sometimes, when we are in the grip of an intense and escalating fight with our partner, our brain is like a runaway train going straight downhill. Those mental brakes will be smoking and almost worn through with the effort of stopping the emotional energy surge—and *that's* if we are stone cold sober. Here's what happens when we are inebriated. We flip a switch and that part of the brain just...turns...off. There's no thoughtful conductor to even try to apply the brakes. He's gone to the sleeping coach and is snoring away. Without the tempering influence of the thoughtful part of our brain, we are almost guaranteed to do or say something that will cause enormous damage to the other person and ourselves.

There's another reason why alcohol, in particular, is an impediment to our safe navigation of the divorce transition. Alcohol is a depressant. Literally, it promotes a depressed state of mind. If you have even the slightest tendency toward depression, the combination of divorce and alcohol could not be more personally destructive. A person simply cannot make good decisions for themselves and take care of their own future if they are depressed. A depressed person has a seriously skewed view of the future. In order to prepare for the future, a realistic and clear-eyed view of that future is necessary. We know you can't drink to excess and drive. Nor can you drink to excess and thrive—particularly if you are hooked into chronic, escalating intimate conflict.

Domestic Abuse

Few behaviors set off judicial alarm bells like domestic abuse. Protections for victims are embedded in the laws of each state, and a culture that once shrugged and winked at this behavior now has zero tolerance. That does not mean that victims are secure, as a court order is but a piece of paper and the determined abuser will exact his damage. However, it is important to differentiate two different kinds of domestic violence, because one is far more insidious and dangerous than the other. It is also an insuperable barrier to resolution in divorce.

First, we must consider the couple that is volatile. They engage in reciprocal escalation of conflict until one wishes to disengage because the brain is becoming overwhelmingly flooded. The other equally flooded person cannot tolerate this cutoff and prevents the other from disengaging. Things can become physical in a flash. The violent partner will be punished by legal institutions, as well he or she should be. However, this kind of violence is the product of mutual escalation of conflict.

The more disturbing form of domestic abuse is characterized by a campaign of power and control of one partner over the other. Usually it's the man who exercises this control, and he is frightening. He is angry if she has friends. He controls the money. He is consistently critical of her and can be furious about minor mistakes. He will break things or put his hand through a door in anger. There is an atmosphere of intimidation and complete control. When the abuse becomes physical, she has either been broken or is soon to be. There is no adequate way to describe the fear that dogs her every thought. This abuse is also very secret. There are many excellent resources that describe the dynamic and offer support and routes to safety for the victim of this kind of domestic terrorism. It is not overly dramatic to dub this behavior "terrorism." Whatever impairment resides inside the brain of the domestic abuser, it results in the threat to the physical safety of the victim and their children. It is imperative that she (and it is almost always a "she") seek out support in her community. The law *absolutely* recognizes the desperate need for her to escape and for her whereabouts to remain secret.

Marriage to an abuser creates both fear and shame. It is often not something willingly shared, even with those who are there to help. Professionals are trained to make appropriate inquiries, and it is extremely important that this critical information not be withheld. One of the characteristics of domestic abuse is the isolation of the abused partner. There is a systematic effort to separate the victim from all sources of support—friends, families, and professionals. One must reach out, however, if they are going to deal with this enormous life challenge. If the threat of "crossing" your spouse and angering him is a significant fear, you must share that with your support system— your close friend, therapist, and doctor. This is not something that can be faced alone.

COUPLES WORK
FINDING AN APPROACH THAT WORKS FOR YOU

If you are going somewhere for the first time, you need a map or GPS. If you have neither, then when you hit State Highway 187, you'll have no idea if you are on track or completely lost. That is why a strong supportive theory of couples intervention and change is essential if you want to avoid a haphazard process that may fizzle out or explode when you end up at a dead end. As mentioned early in this book, many smart, insightful practitioners have developed approaches to healing couples in distress.

These different theories help the struggling couple achieve balance and reconnection. As an initial task, all approaches seek to lower the intensity of conflict and the attendant lack of safety in the relationship. The steps that follow may be generally seen as helping people in intimate relationships find a way to say what they've got to say to each other. Different approaches promote different ways to do that. Each uses a different language.

John and Julie Gottman have a well-respected approach organized around their notion of the "Sound Marital House." Their work is the product of decades of observing couples in distress and at peace. The Gottman Theory provides a clearly defined roadmap of behaviors and their rationales which lead to a deeper intimate connection. Harville Hendrix and Helen Lakely Hunt have developed a dynamic approach which they call Imago Therapy. Their approach is beautifully summarized in Hendrix' classic, *Getting the Love You Want*. The Imago Therapist helps the struggling individual explore the impact of their earliest relationships with parental figures and the efforts being made now to heal those early wounds in the current relationship. David Schnarch, a well-regarded expert in human sexuality and Ruth Morehouse developed Crucible Therapy which enhances sexual connection and intimacy through promoting personal growth and "differentiation" in each partner. Terry Real has developed an approach to couples work which he shares in his many writings, workshops and the Relational Life Institute. I recently had dinner with a couple of colleagues who had attended one of his workshops and their enthusiasm filled the room and bounced off the walls. Brent Atkinson has developed an approach to couples work that concentrates in managing the intense emotional brain-states triggered by marital conflict.

Explanatory websites for these, and other leading approaches can be found in the Appendix. My observation is that each of these therapies describe a common problem and set of solutions in different languages. Practitioners are drawn to the language which most appeals to them and their intuitive sense of how things work for people in relationship. The enthusiasm I described over Real's work is matched by the verve displayed by those who *connect* with Gottman, Hendrix, Schnarch, Perel, Atkinson, Bader, Tatkin, Wile and the rest.

The approach that forms the foundation of my own training is Emotionally Focused Couples Therapy. It is the language that I respond to. It *makes sense* to me and, therefore, much of what will follow reflects this language.

Emotionally Focused Therapy (or EFT) rests on a foundation of attachment. The need of the infant for connection with attuned, consistent caregivers, that lies deep within our brains, is the drive for attachment. We never "grow out of" that need – it just transfers from parental figures to our closest adult relationships. While attachment needs are met to varying degrees by our close friends, relatives and others, nobody will both satisfy that inherent yearning *and* destabilize us profoundly with its withholding as much as our intimate partner. While we don't put all our eggs in that emotional basket, the ones we leave out won't make much of an omelet.

EFT views each person in a distressed couple as reacting to the insecurity of their attachment bond. If we view this need as central to our basic sense of wellbeing, then a disturbance in that force will cause the internal vibrations we call anxiety to start shakin', rattlin', and rollin' in each partner. The greater the threat to wellbeing, the more intense the anxiety. The more intense the anxiety, the more each person will began to react emotionally to the other. By "react" I am describing an instantaneous, emotionally-driven set of feelings, thoughts and behaviors that will overtake the couple. This faster-than-the-speed-of-light dance consisting of mutual, emotional, reactivity is called a "cycle" by EFT therapists. It is almost always beyond the conscious awareness of the two people caught in its grasp, as the couple enters the therapist's office with concrete complaints about sex, childrearing, money, household chores, and the like. The "process" that we attend to in EFT is the cycle.

Virtually every couple's cycle will consist of one partner who tends to be an emotional *pursuer* and the other, who is an emotional *withdrawer.* The pursuer is the partner with greater awareness of the status of the relationship and emotional availability of their partner. The withdrawer is usually less conscious of, or concerned with, the status of the relationship until it is perceived that their partner is **un-happy.** A dissatisfied partner is profoundly destabilizing for the withdrawer, just as an emotionally disconnected partner is destabilizing for the pursuer. This is as true with the *apparently* dissatisfied partner and the *apparently* disconnected partner.

Years of research and reports from experienced EFT practitioners reveal that emotional pursuers, when anxious and caught up in the cycle, tend to describe their experience as feeling:

- Hurt
- Alone
- Deprived
- Desperate
- Invisible
- Abandoned

Emotional withdrawers, when anxious and caught up in the cycle tend to describe their experience as feeling:

- Rejected
- Inadequate
- Numb-Frozen
- Judged or Criticized
- Ashamed
- Empty

So how do people who struggle with these feelings interact in a cycle? Well, it doesn't matter where it starts—it can begin with the pursuer or the withdrawer—but let's start with the pursuer, here. Winston does something or says something (or *doesn't* do something or say something) that causes Pauline to feel unimportant and un-cared-for by him. Maybe she had experienced this for a long time and just let it pass, thinking that time would work its magic, and Winston's seeming lack of care is either not so important (and she'd learn to live with it) or an aberration (and he would come around). She might make comments here or there expressing her dissatisfaction or concern. These complaints would be experienced by Winston as little stones in his shoes and he'd let them slide, though they made him uncomfortable.

At some point in the relationship (it could be a month in or after 10 years or more), Pauline will more aggressively pursue Winston for connection. She would not feel at all safe telling him how scared and abandoned she feels (she may not even be aware of this underlying feeling) but she *will* let him know what he isn't doing or what he should do differently so that she won't be so unhappy and (usually) so *angry*. Anger, in our culture, doesn't render us as vulnerable as expressions of fear, sadness or shame and since Pauline is seriously wondering if Winston even cares for her, she isn't about to open up to him in this risky manner.

Winston is deeply bruised by Pauline's dissatisfaction and anger. He wants her to be happy and he *definitely* wants her to be happy with *him*. When she lets him know how unhappy she is the first thing he is likely to do is either defend himself or retreat for safety. This relationship is causing him to feel inadequate and who wants to feel that? So Winston will withdraw. He can withdraw into self-defense or silence or the television/computer or into a bottle or to the office. There are many different avenues of withdrawal.

Is this what Pauline is seeking? No, it is the opposite. Thus, Pauline will amp up her complaints, trying to get Winston to understand her distress. Yet the more and louder Pauline complains, the more Winston will withdraw. Each reacts to the other until the pursuer can become either so chronically furious or exhausted and shut down, and the withdrawer can harden his protective shell to the point of complete emotional disengagement and numbness, that when they walk into a couples therapist's office they are alienated and deeply dispirited.

The Emotionally Focused Therapist meets these people in this very painful place and the first task is to put both people at ease. There can never be a time in which either person believes the therapist is more sympathetic or aligned with their partner. There are times when a word or action by the therapist might threaten the connection with a client, but these will be addressed and put to rest in the client's mind as quickly as possible.

The next step, after creating this safe space and then gathering basic history, is to explore the nature of this couple's cycle. The exploration may take a few meetings, but the goal is to identify what happens inside Pauline when she experiences Winston's disconnection. What does he do that triggers her? When he does these things, what does she make of this behavior—what does it say to her about how he feels about her? When she comes to these conclusions, what does she experience emotionally and how does she share this with Winston? Because these steps operate at the speed of our synapses, Pauline can go from Winston's gesture or comment all the way through that process to spitting out some pained, and painful, statement in less than a second. The same is true on Winston's side, as well.

When we think of our intimate relationships as vital to our basic sense of wellbeing, we can easily understand the rapid snap of reaction to a threat to this relationship and the security of our bond. This is an excellent example of Einstein's adage at work, because people do not enter a couples therapist's office with an awareness of their cycle. They are much more aware of their fight over how much sex they are (or aren't) having or who is spending too much and who is sucking the joy out of life by proposing an unreasonable budget. It takes time, and there will be advances and retreats along the path, but the goal is for the couple to start coming into the therapist's office and say, "We almost got into a cycle two nights ago, but we saw it was happening and nipped it in the bud."

As the work progresses, the goal is to help the pursuer see, and accept, that she really is loved by and deeply valued by her withdrawer partner. We also work to help the withdrawer understand that his pursuer partner is not destructive or impossible to satisfy or crazy but is trying to gain a security with him that she dares not even admit she needs, much less allow herself to believe it can be achieved in this relationship.

The profound, and moving, part of this work occurs when each partner begins to slowly trust in the safety of the other's heart. It is something that has usually been there all along, but the cycle has kicked up such a storm of dust that the truth has been obscured, often for years. The relationship is transformed. When the heart speaks honestly from its place of need and vulnerability, trust is restored. People sink into the arms—and the hearts—of each other in ways they might have never experienced before. Old pains can be shared and heard, *for the first time*, without defensiveness. Physical intimacy and sexual exploration reenters the relationship, if it had been AWOL over time. Our partner makes a seemingly miraculous transformation from a label to a person. (For an excellent summary of the EFT process, I invite you to look at the roadmap prepared by Veronica Kallos-Lilly and Pat LaDouceur, which is in the Appendix.)

Sue Johnson's research has suggested that this process can take as little as twenty sessions, although most experienced EFT therapists believe it is more realistic to see this as a longer process. Multiple studies have shown that over 70% of couples experience significant relief from intimate distress and remain satisfied long afterward.

One thing I have loved about this work is to have the repeated experience of reading deeply about something and then *seeing it happen* right in front of me. Everybody who does enough of something will not only see the stuff they've read confirmed, but there will also be personal observations that reflect one's own filters and ideas. That's what the next chapter is about.

TAKEAWAYS

- **Seeing a couples therapist is not a sign of failure or weakness. Couples in serious or long-term distress, if left to their own devices, will probably blow apart. Each person has already tried everything they knew how to do to fix things.**
- **Changing—healing—a relationship requires a completely different way of thinking about the other person *and* the relationship.**
- **Be thoughtful about your search for a couples therapist. Read what they say about themselves and their approach on their website. Almost every therapist these days projects themselves as a couples counselor. Take advantage of**

the information they provide. Never go blindly into a therapeutic relationship. Seek to understand this person's approach and see if it (1) is specifically focused on working with couples and (2) makes sense to you. If possible, get a referral from friends who have worked with some one they *both* liked

CHAPTER 3

Seven Observations of Couples in Therapy

Dennis and Cathy

Dennis sat in Norma's waiting room, casually browsing *People* magazine. He only read it here and at the doctor's office, but, as he and Cathy joked sometimes, how was he going to manage a cocktail party without "loading up on *People*?" Cathy was running a little late; her tardiness had irritated him since their first date, when he had to cool his heels on the couch and make small talk to her small-talking, boring roommate for fifteen minutes. Dennis felt it was incredibly disrespectful to be late and never managed to understand how Cathy *didn't* understand that. Cathy was always blithe about it and thought Dennis should "chill." He had learned to let go of it, concluding, with Norma's help, that Cathy wasn't going to change and, most importantly, that her lax attitude about punctuality didn't make her a basically inconsiderate person. Then again, that hadn't been the big, almost deal-breaking problem that had driven them into Norma's office nine months ago as a bitter, angry, and disconnected couple. No, it had been his inability to handle Cathy's sudden rages. Talk about "walking on eggshells!" He had felt this way for two or three years before they saw Norma as a last try at couples therapy. They had seen two people before Norma over the years. The first seemed kind of clueless, and the two of them would get into a fight in the office and just get upset, leaving the sessions more wound up than they had been an hour earlier. The second was more in control of the sessions, but after a couple of months, Cathy was convinced that he was on Dennis's side and wanted to stop coming. That was particularly frustrating to Dennis, because it was the first time someone had said directly to Cathy that she had to stop being so angry at him for inconsequential things. He had thought, "Finally, someone other than me is saying these things to Cathy." A lot of good that did him! Cathy blew out of therapy not long after that and Dennis, at that point, made a decision to just shut up and try avoiding her blasts. That was the best he would get out of this marriage.

However, they had experienced their biggest blowout just before they found Norma, in a state of desperation. They knew this was going to be the last shot and if they didn't fix things, he was done. He might have been done, anyway. He walked around the house angry almost all the time, just waiting for another fight from out of nowhere. If he kept his head down and his mouth shut, he would manage to keep it fairly quiet. No question, though, that his energies had turned increasingly outward from the marriage. Work, friendships, the gym—these had been his respite from the worst part of his life, which was home. Then Cathy had pulled her dramatic stunt when Gabe had come to visit, disappearing for an entire week to be with Mary Jane. She didn't call or come by, and Gabe never saw her. Rather than hang out and have the good time he had been planning, Dennis spent the long weekend talking with Gabe about whether he'd get divorced. After that week, when he said he couldn't do this anymore, Cathy jerked back as if struck and had tearfully asked for one last chance. He had reluctantly agreed to try one more marriage therapist. He had heard about the first edition of this book by Joseph Shaub and picked it up. Dennis decided to try Emotionally Focused Therapy. Cathy had agreed and found Norma Ramierez after a web search.

One strange thing at the beginning was Norma's asking if she could video record their sessions for her own review later. She said she often missed things in the sessions and it was helpful to go back over portions or whole sessions later. She also had a consultant therapist she shared cases and recordings with, and she said it was like "getting two therapists for the price of one." She made it seem natural, and he and Cathy had surprisingly agreed—surprising for him, particularly, as he was such a private person. As Norma had predicted, the small camera off to the side soon disappeared from his awareness. The other thing he remembers about the first meeting was that she asked questions about what had worked in the relationship—why they had been attracted to each other in the first place. Boy, he hadn't thought about that in a long time and, even though it was hard to muster much "oomph" from any positive memories, he had to concede to himself that there had once been something more between them than silence and explosions. In his eyes, she was still a beautiful woman, and he had always appreciated the care she took in how she looked. Until she had started to make him feel guilty for spending time with his friends, he hadn't resented her and had enjoyed his time with her—at least when they went on vacation together.

Finally, Norma wanted to hear about their latest fight—what had happened and in what sequence. That wasn't as hard as the other, since he and Cathy had been pissed at each other just the night before, when he wanted to reschedule the first session because he had a brief he had to complete and was running behind. Cathy had told him that all he thought about was himself. He got angry that she was calling him selfish because he had to work. That one was constant and it *still* made no sense! She had to stop resenting him for the thing that had bought her their beautiful house and that ring on her finger she loved so much. He thought that he could survive in this marriage if he just kept his mouth shut and stayed out of the line of fire—but that hadn't worked, and he just blew. He'd thrown a glass across the room and it shattered against the wall. "My God, Cathy, will you just shut up!" he had yelled. "If you want to bitch about me, go do it somewhere else. Go call your mother—you said she doesn't like me, anyway. You know, Gabe is right. You are a borderline. Your therapy isn't working and all those pills you take certainly aren't working. You've got a beautiful house, a great kid, a husband who doesn't cheat or abuse you, and you just complain all the goddamn time!" Cathy had then pointed to the mark left by the wine on the wall where the glass had exploded and replied, with eyes closed to slits, "You don't think *that* is emotional abuse? Fuck you, Dennis. You don't know what you're talking about. You scare me." She then retreated to the bedroom, locked the door, and they spent the night separately, barely sleeping.

He remembers Norma seeming sympathetic to him and saying something like, "So, Dennis, when you threw that wine glass, it sounds like you felt helpless to affect Cathy's feelings about you. She was just going to think you were a selfish jerk and there was nothing you could do about that, huh?" He remembers nodding and thinking, "Goddamn right!" "Yeah," Norma had said, "that's a tough place to be." "But he *is* a jerk sometimes!" said Cathy, her voice approaching a whine. Norma turned to her and said, "And you try to get through to him, get him to understand that his constant preoccupation with work and other things makes you feel that he is just gone. It hurts and makes you angry to feel abandoned like that." Cathy had let out a long breath, said in a low voice, "Yes," and sat back on the couch.

Norma had spent several months talking to them about a "cycle" that would "sweep them up" and that it didn't matter what they were arguing about—the cycle always overtook them with the speed of light and, before they knew it, a fragile peace would explode in anger, with verbal grenades flying back and forth.

Norma had given them homework which, unlike their other therapists' homework, didn't direct them to change anything or act differently. It was more to become aware of what was happening when it was happening. Norma would explain, "Your cycle starts so fast and ramps up so quickly that you don't realize that you are each going through a number of steps instantaneously. You hear or see what the other does; you draw conclusions about their behavior (which almost always has something to do with how the other is disconnected or unsafe or doesn't care); you then react to that belief (to protect yourself from how bad that belief of yours feels); and then your partner goes through the same process. Slow it down if you can. Become more aware of your own triggers and what is going on inside of you then. We'll be talking about that a fair amount for a while." Norma told them that the first, and primary, goal at the beginning was to make their home feel safer—to lower the intensity and frequency of the conflicts. It took a few months, and some solid, helpful sessions with Norma, before he was able to get the hang of it from his end.

Cathy knew she was emotional. In a lot of ways, she liked that about herself. Still, from the time she was little, she had felt embarrassed—even ashamed—at how upset things would get her. Her mother had been the guiding light of her life. She was already successful as a marketing executive when Cathy had been born. Cathy had idolized her mother, who was beautiful, charismatic, and steady as a rock. When Cathy was in college and saw a counselor for the first time for depression, she had described her mother as "loving and kind." When asked to give examples of this, Cathy had readily unspooled stories about her mother's almost legendary acts of magnanimity to people in her life—but there seemed to be a vacuum where attention to Cathy would have been. Still, Cathy would assure this therapist, and others to come, that her mother had a lot of responsibilities. Her parents hadn't fought and she remembers her family home as almost idyllic—the "almost" being injected by her older brother, Cal, who she recalls as being mean to her from the start. While Cathy was the "good girl," Cal had been the surly troublemaker. When Cathy would get dressed up as a little girl for a party or for church, Cal wouldn't miss a chance to tell her how ugly she was. She recalled the many times he would put her down, damage something in her room (and claim innocence), or try to get their parents angry at her. Once, when he was twelve and she was eight, he wrestled her to the ground and, with his hands on her shoulders, arms extended, he leaned over her face and let drools of spit fall onto her eyes and lips. He started smoking weed at thirteen and barely got out of high school. When she told her dad about Cal, he'd sit her brother down for a half-hearted heart-to-heart, but it would all just continue. She just stayed away from her brother, but she was always frightened of him. Her mom was like a beautiful ice princess—kind, strong, and, at the same time, distant. A lot of the family's attention went to the troubled Cal while Cathy was left to her own devices. She was reliable and didn't cause any trouble. She was a real gift to her parents.

From an early age, Cathy knew she'd never measure up to her mother. She grew from a pretty young girl into a beautiful woman and the attention she received from men, starting in adolescence, was the only power she ever felt she had. She did well enough in school to get into a nursing program and she was working as an RN when she had met this smart, smooth, and extremely attractive and self-possessed young lawyer named Dennis. She had fallen in love with him by their second date. He reminded her a bit of her mother. There didn't seem to be a challenge he couldn't meet or a person that didn't come away impressed by him in some way. She could build a life with him, and he did not have one tiny iota of the cruelty that she had experienced in Cal and that she feared resided in all men.

The honeymoon didn't even last until the honeymoon. She found her relationship with Dennis to be far more vertiginous a ride then she had expected. They would go through a period of intense connection—usually when they were away together on vacation—and then they would blow up and be upset for days or even a week or two at a time. She loved Dennis deeply, but he would go through these periods when he was just beyond her grasp. He'd disappear into himself. Those would be the times when she would get angry at him. Sure, she admitted, she screamed at him to rattle his cage sometimes. She'd do *anything* to get his attention. He would usually just look at her with exasperation and get hyper-logical. "What do you want me to do, Cathy?" he'd ask in this put-upon tone. When he did that, she wanted to slap him. She never did, but that didn't keep her from letting him know how self-centered he was. Dennis was more interested in how everyone else felt about him, and he sure did put a lot of energy into making sure he was universally well liked. She told Mary Jane once that "Dennis is my mom with balls. Come to think of it, my mom has balls, too. Okay, he's my mom with a dick." She and Mary Jane would laugh about this over wine during their mutual commiseration sessions.

Their first marriage therapist was a disaster. Cathy would try to get him and Dennis to understand how hard it was to be married to someone as narcissistic as Dennis (she had read about narcissists and thought that fit Dennis to a "T"). Dennis would look aggravated and tell her that therapy was not going to be a "dump on Dennis" session, the way things worked at home. That would wind Cathy up and the therapist would sit there like a deer in the headlights. So much for him!

A couple of years later, they tried again, but this one *really* didn't get it. It was a "dump on Cathy" session as the therapist would seem irritated at her whenever she tried to explain how self-centered Dennis was. The therapist was so biased in favor of Dennis—just like everybody else in their life—that he became completely worthless to Cathy by the third session.

Dennis kept telling her to get therapy, like their problems were all her fault. Their good times together seemed to get jammed into tinier and tinier spaces, and the nasty fights and subsequent arctic winters expanded to pretty nearly fill their lives. She had tried antidepressants, but they hadn't worked and she stopped taking them. Dennis enjoyed other people more than he enjoyed her. She even found herself becoming jealous whenever Dennis would go off and do something with their son, Logan. She began to worry if Dennis was setting her up to divorce her and take their seven-year-old son.

Over the last four years she had been calling her mother more and seeking out advice. She had divorced Cathy's dad when Cathy was fourteen, and she needed to know what the signs might be that Dennis was out the door. Her mother, who still worked a demanding schedule and was still striking in appearance and manner, would give her advice but became frustrated with Cathy when she couldn't follow through on her suggestions. She had told Cathy, for example, to consider going back to school or developing a career of her own, now that Logan was in school, but Cathy couldn't imagine not being there for her son.

One thing Cathy became conscious of was Dennis's way of talking down to her. For a sweet-seeming guy, he was one of the most judgmental people she had ever known...*the* most judgmental! He would tell her there was something wrong with her, like she was flawed, when she would be late (which she had to admit, happened a lot) or when she would get angry when he came home after dinner for the *fourth straight night,* blaming a court deadline. That was why she had finally lost it when his friend Gabe came to visit. "Enough," she had said to herself. He knew how important it was for them to connect. He knew how much she had been looking forward to dinner at Cormier's. She had told him this wasn't a good time for Gabe to come because the two of them needed more time together. Still, he set it up, probably purposely, to miss Cormier's, and that had been the last straw.

Yet, when she had come back from the week at Mary Jane's, expecting him to be conciliatory (after all, she *had* stayed out of the way and given him his precious time with Gabe) he had shocked her by saying he was through. After the quick wave of shock and anger, she panicked. She had begged him for one more chance (which in retrospect had made her feel ashamed and resentful) and found a therapist who had an approach that was supposed to be effective with couples like them. She did a little research into emotionally focused therapy, and found Norma Ramierez.

Cathy had liked Norma. She had at first balked at the camera, but after the third session had relented and soon it was a nonissue. Norma didn't make Cathy feel embarrassed or weak when she talked about Dennis being selfish. When she talked about being so lonely she felt sometimes like she was choking, Norma understood. She was safe with her and, even though Dennis was sitting on the other end of the couch, the conversations a lot of times seemed to be just between her and Norma. Norma would periodically turn to Dennis and ask him what he was experiencing after Cathy had shared a particularly painful fear or talked about being so sure he would leave that she went a little crazy sometimes. Norma talked about this "cycle" that would grab her and Dennis's relationship, like some external malevolent force, and bathe them both in such fear and need for protection that they each forgot about the other or at least how much their own behavior hurt the other. Cathy slowly began to gain an inkling that she had a great impact on Dennis and that, far from his being completely uncaring, he was quite sensitive to almost everything she said to him. He once said that he needed to make himself "numb" in order to tolerate Cathy's blasts of anger. During one potentially explosive argument, Cathy was able to stop herself from feeling defensive, and she even got a small sense of how shaken Dennis was by her expressions of intense dissatisfaction. He even had tears in his eyes, which she hadn't seen in...well, forever. It didn't take Cathy long after that brief insight to return to her basic doubt that Dennis could really, truly be vulnerable to anything she said to him. Yet, that first time felt like a tiny seed had been planted in her, and she had experienced a small, but definite, shift. Their fights started to become less frequent. She still had tons of doubt about whether this could work, but after about three months with Norma, the temperature had been dialed down a notch, and that felt like a relief to her.

PERSONAL OBSERVATIONS

Have you ever studied something and then, when you did it yourself, that moment would come when you saw with your own eyes what the teachers had been talking about? If so, you can appreciate the fun and amazement I experience every time the cycle plays out in my office. I have often said to myself, "Son of a gun! That's just the way the books, or the trainers, said it happens." The living part reinforces the reading-about part. My father would always say, "Don't reinvent the wheel," but he was wrong. We all have to reinvent the wheel for ourselves. We can hear about something over and over (especially when we are young), but we can't believe it, absorb it into our cells, unless we experience it ourselves. Then, we can make it our own, even if it has been an experience or observation shared by millions over time.

Over the years, I've made my own observations of people in relationship therapy that underscore the teaching of others. These are my own wheels, carved with my own hands, seen with my own eyes, marveled at by my own mind.

OBSERVATION NO. 1
WHAT YOU THINK YOU'RE TALKING ABOUT ISN'T WHAT YOU'RE TALKING ABOUT

Nancy has been the sole bread winner for the past eight years as Roger took time off from his work as an architect in order to be a house-husband for their three sons. Now she is extremely burned out and way over-burdened. She has told him for the past two years that he needs to go back to work. He reasonably tries to explain to her that work is hard to come by in his field because of the recession and, if he went back to work, the childcare costs would strip away much of what he would earn. Nancy becomes furious and laces into Roger who, of course, complains about the terrible things she says about him. Roger and Nancy think they are talking about her need for him to get back to work and his complaints about her nasty temper. Yet, the fear in her eyes belies her fury, and the desperation with which he tries to explain himself to her hints at how much her regard matters to him. They're not talking about that, though.

Judy seems to come totally unglued whenever Marty smiles at a waitress, a flight attendant, or any other attractive woman they come across. She is sure that he is attracted to other women, but when he denies this, she feels like he is trying to make her crazy. He gets angry when he tells her how he is feeling, but she won't believe him and accuses him of many things that are just not who he is. It's affecting their small children, who get exposed to the fights. He's come to the point when he doesn't want to even engage in these conversations any more, and, predictably, Judy takes his shutting down all discussion as insensitive at best and proof of guilt at worst. Judy's past has left her sensitive about feeling unlovable. The shame she experiences at these times seems to swallow her up, and she desperately needs Marty's reassurance. Sadly, Marty came from a background in which he was constantly made to feel bad for being or doing things that he was not or had not. He has searing memories of punishments that far outstripped his childhood crimes. The pain of her "unfair" condemnation makes him clamp down like an oyster to protect himself even while he wants to make her feel loved and protected. They're not talking about that, though.

Stan has worked hard to build up his business, providing alternative energy consultation to local small businesses. When oil prices continued to climb, his customer list followed, enabling his family to enjoy annual trips, private school, and other perks of business success. His wife, Sally, met Stan in college, and although she could have had a good career in HR, she left work two years after graduation. They married six months before the first of their two children was born. Sally throws all of her intelligence and drive into parenting, and she has been president of the PTSA and organized many enrichment activities for her kids. But she feels she's doing it all alone. She hardly ever sees Stan and, when she does, it's invariably disappointing. The minute he walks in the door, he doesn't want to talk and gets angry when she presses the issue and wants to talk about the kids. This angry man is not who she married and she feels deceived. There's something wrong with him. She's been reading about Narcissistic Personality Disorder and a lot of it sounds *exactly* like Stan. He is spending more and more time at work ("where people *like* me") and away from Sally's increasingly "shrewish" behavior.

Sally had been the perfect latchkey child. Both parents worked and she, as the oldest of four kids, was dutifully responsible. She learned at an early age that, while she'd always have food on the table and a roof over her head, she was basically on her own when emotional needs were involved. She has always had a strong circle of friends and hoped Stan would be a friend. Instead, she feels a crazy split—on one hand she needs to know she can lean on him if she gets scared or overwhelmed, but on the other, she hates the very idea of letting herself get to that place. She doesn't know how to ask to be taken care of, so she gets angry. Stan came from a high-achieving family, and his two brothers are much more successful and wealthier than he is. It eats at him that not only his family, but his own wife doesn't seem to appreciate what he has accomplished. It makes him feel alone and hopeless when he is with his family. They're not talking about that, though.

Finally, Dean and Sylvia are in the tenth year of the second marriage for each. They met and fell in love while still married to their first spouses. When they got together, Dean made a lot of unilateral decisions, from the architect for their home remodel, to where they'd go to dinner on weekends when all five kids came to stay with them. She gets more and more worried about his controlling tendencies, so like her mother's; Sylvia has fought with her mom since she emerged from the womb. While everyone has loved Sylvia's free-spiritedness throughout her life, Dean gets angry if she wants to make eleventh-hour changes to plans. They're not sure they can stay married, because she is "way too flaky" and he is "an emotional abuser." However, Dean's judgments of Sylvia hurt her deeply. She was constantly criticized by her anxious and angry mother, and Dean's hard looks send her right back into those feelings of defectiveness. Dean's family growing up was just as chaotic as Sylvia's was rigid and organized.

When life feels like it is not predictable, his world begins to feel out of control, which makes him off-balance and nervous. His stomach gets upset and he sleeps poorly. Only when he can re-impose order by making decisions does he start to calm down and feel okay. They're not talking about that, though.

Certain couples therapists share a great term: we need to avoid "going down the content tube." Couples come in, and they always (always, always) have the things they are fighting about. No couple is without their content.

She wants him to *finally* go back to work, but he believes she doesn't understand what that means to the family and is being unreasonable. They spend forever debating this. She says he is always flirting and he doesn't know how much that kills her, but he gets exasperated because it just isn't true and she won't believe him. For years each has tried to get the other to understand how reasonable their position is, to no avail. She keeps bugging him for not being around, "but she sure doesn't complain when we go to Hawaii every year." She despairs because she can't get him to understand that it's easier for her to be alone *if she were alone* than "being in this sham marriage." They talk about these issues like they are arguing to an imaginary jury. The jury always gets hung up, and the couple never gets the verdict they seek.

Many people come into couples therapy certain that they are the one who is reasonable—that a third person will finally vindicate them, that this trained professional will see that they are rightfully hurt and angry, and the therapist, with all their education and experience, will finally find the way to explain things to their spouse so they'll hear it. The only problem is that both people come in with the same need and agenda. The transformative realization is that it's not about the content of their argument. This fight is a dead end—guaranteed. It's a debate with a frightened, defensive, and emotional adversary. Nothing good will come of it. Yet, if they can talk about what lies underneath all that stuff, they will find a way of working the content arguments out.

What people in intimate conflict long to get worked out is their connection. They desperately want to re-establish safety. One might feel his partner actually hates him, but, almost always, that's simply not true. Another might feel she lives in constant fear that he might not really love her and she is truly alone in this world, but that's not nearly true either. Some couples therapy is pretty easy, helping people see that their old fears about the way the other feels just isn't so. Lots of couples therapy is more challenging and takes time. Our deepest fears and vulnerabilities are *deep* for a good reason. For all the success in showing the world a smart, poised, successful, attractive person, if anyone saw these kernels of doubt buried within our hearts, we could be wiped out. Who'd want to risk that unless we were certain this other person was safe (which right now they are most definitely *not*)? You sure wouldn't—nor should you.

So people spin around arguing about the other stuff and go down one dead end after another.

OBSERVATION NO. 2
LABELS BELONG ON PRODUCTS,
NOT YOUR PARTNER

An interesting phenomenon occurs when the cycle is left to spin and spin and grow and grow. Not only are we more likely to do and say things that are deeply wounding and will need time and care to heal, we also get into labeling.

June and Robert stand before 200 of their family members and friends. She looks lovely in her mother's wedding dress, and he beams as he gazes at her. The minister says, "June, do you take this Narcissist as your lawfully wedded husband?" Her eyes brim with tears of sweet joy and she almost whispers, "Yes." He turns to the man and says, "Robert, do you take this hysterical *insane* woman as your lawfully wedded wife?" Robert mutters, "Finally," to a wave of chuckles from the crowd and says, "I do." "Good, I now pronounce you over-controlling asshole and bitch goddess of the world."

People in the throes of intimate combat will say the only reason this didn't happen was because their eyes were so glazed over with love and lust that they couldn't see the truth. Well, *that's* not so. Labels are just the product of heightened stress caused by escalating conflict. You don't hang a label on your partner, or hurl a wounding comment at them right after you say, "Honey, please pass the peas." Labels come from the same place that phrases like "you always" and "you never" come from. They are more reflective of the speaker's distress than they are a statement of clear observation and truth.

Hanging a label is another example of the win/lose dynamic of dead-end intimate conflict. Obviously, if you can put your partner in a box and define them as mentally ill or deficient in some way, it will help you *win*. Because, make no mistake, in these kinds of fights, if *you win, I lose*. When couples are caught in an escalating cycle, they lose sight of the idea that they can both be right—that my win doesn't mean your loss. More importantly, your win doesn't mean *I* have to lose.

When intimate battle reduces down to each person trying desperately to gain the advantage so they are not wrong, any maneuver will work. Deciding that the other person is basically defective in some way is a strong buffer against being wrong.

OBSERVATION NO. 3
YOU ARE CERTAINLY DIFFERENT;
YOU'RE PROBABLY NOT INCOMPATIBLE

Many is the time when one or both people in a stressed-out relationship will look at me with certainty and say, "We're just incompatible." I imagine a round of kettle drums ushering in the forces of doom. That's quite a proclamation, after all. I believe that conclusion is another example of the oft-demonstrated rule: When left to their own devices, couples in chronic conflict will usually blow apart. Here, a calmer outsider is needed to let them know that this is simply not true. Being different doesn't mean incompatibility. To be sure, differences that each person believes are incredibly important—so that demonstrations of these differences cause anger and frustration—will place tremendous stress on the relationship until they are worked out.

One person hates being late, saying it is disrespectful of other people. The other says that he is late because there is a lot to do to get ready; anyway, lots of people are late and it's not the end of the world. "You're selfish and disorganized," says one. "You're uptight and take the fun out of things," responds the other. *We're incompatible.*

One person believes that children need discipline and organization if they are going to succeed. If that means parents have to ride them to make sure they get everything done, then that's the parents' job. The other disagrees, saying kids need to learn the value of self-discipline to succeed in life. If they screw around and get a bad grade, that is going to teach them values. "You are lazy and don't have high enough standards for our children," claims one. "You are OCD and you're going to cripple our kids because they won't know how to make it on their own," says the other. *We're incompatible.*

One person wants to take every spare penny after paying for essentials and put it in savings. Security is defined by some money in the bank and a solid retirement. The other believes that "you only live once" and is feeling starved by the disagreements they have every time he wants to do something that costs anything. "You are irresponsible and immature in the way you deal with money," comes the accusation. "Life with you has become boring. We never do anything," is the defense. *We're incompatible.*

One person likes to experiment sexually. Fantasy, being tied up, catching a quickie in a semi-public place is a turn on. The other enjoys sex—conventional sex, at home, with the same kind of slow foreplay, ending with intercourse in one of a couple of positions. "You are uptight and I'm feeling my sexual interest waning," moans the first. "You pressure me about sex a lot and it isn't any fun with you," responds the other. *We're incompatible.*

One person wants to live close to her family. She has two brothers and a sister, all of whom live in the same part of town as their parents. The other doesn't have much of a relationship with his own family of origin and would like to live on the other side of the country from any family members so he and his wife can have their own life. "You want to take me away from my family. You're a loner and want me to be one, too," is the main complaint. "You are enmeshed with your family and it isn't healthy. Why don't you want to strengthen *our* family?" is the inevitable retort. *We're incompatible.*

And on and on it goes. Differences abound with the outgoing and the withdrawn; the tidy and the sloppy; the optimist and the pessimist; the active recreator and the plant your butt somewhere reader; the socializer and the stay home just the two-of-us-er; or the person who desires more time together and the one who needs more time apart. While it's certainly not unheard of for a couple to find themselves similar in almost all approaches to life, these pairs are a slim minority. The rest of us must learn to cope with differences.

As noted earlier, one of John Gottman's most valuable observations is this: Of all the conflicts experienced by intimate partners (and these can run from the recently married to sixty-year bonds that are strong and universally admired), fully 69% of these differences are perpetual. They'll *never* get resolved. If one says they will move more to the middle if the other does, well, they'll be waiting a long time and will likely grow increasingly angry in the process. Gottman's studies reflected the reality that almost all intimate relationships have their differences, but that doesn't mean people are incompatible. He quotes a wonderful passage, from the wise and humorous couples therapist Daniel Wile, which has been proven true over and over again in my own office:[11]

> *Paul married Alice and Alice gets loud at parties and Paul, who is shy, hates that. But if Paul had married Susan, he and Susan would have gotten into a fight before they even got to the party. That's because Paul is always late and Susan hates to be kept waiting. She would feel taken for granted, which she is very sensitive about. Paul would see her complaining about this as her attempt to dominate him, which he is very sensitive about. If Paul had married Gail, they wouldn't have even gone to the party because they would still be upset about an argument they had the day before about Paul's not helping with the housework. To Gail, when Paul does not help she feels abandoned, which she is sensitive about, and to Paul, Gail's complaining is an attempt at domination, which he is sensitive about. The same is true about Alice. If she had married Steve, she would have the opposite problem, because Steve gets drunk at parties and she would get so angry at his drinking that they would get into a fight about it. If she had married Lou, she*

and Lou would have enjoyed the party but then when they got home the trouble would begin when Lou wanted sex because he always wants sex when he wants to feel closer, but sex is something Alice wants when she already feels close.

...there is value, when choosing a long-term partner, in realizing that you will inevitably be choosing a particular set of unsolvable problems that you'll be grappling with for the next ten, twenty, or fifty years.

The first step toward trouble is when we start to believe that the other person's way of being in the world shows thoughtlessness toward us. "If they really cared, they'd _____." Personalizing basic differences shifts a perfectly fine way of living one's life into something wrong or bad. The natural response to that kind of an accusation is defensiveness. How can one act with equanimity if they are being told that who they are shows that they are selfish and unloving?

Let's step back from that ledge. At this point, it would help to just take a deep breath and accept that we are the way we are for a good reason. Life, after all, is just the ongoing effort to make sense of our world and to feel secure within it. That's easier for some than for others, but it is a challenge we all face to one degree or another. The ongoing debate about whether we are the way we are because of *Nature* (we were born that way) or *Nurture* (our experiences mold us) is pointless. It is both (along with any number of other influences). Is there any doubt that being raised in a devoutly religious family will have a profound influence on us (likely steering us in the direction of devotion or ardent secularism) or that an overbearing father will nudge his son into being either timid and depressed or aggressive and high achieving? Yet studies of identical twins separated at birth have found remarkable similarities in tendency to religious devotion or basic mood, despite vastly different environments.

There are predilections we have at birth that are very compelling. Psychologist and author Robert Karen recounts this story to illustrate the point:[12] Two identical twin brothers are separated at birth and only meet each other in their thirty-ninth year. As Karen relates it,

Both demonstrated conspicuous obsessive-compulsive traits. They were highly preened, religiously punctual, and so anxious about cleanliness they both regularly scrubbed their hands just short of bleeding. When asked to account for his strong traits, the first blamed his mother, noting that throughout the years of his childhood, she had been fanatically well ordered, insisting that everything be returned to its place and that all the clocks be set to the noonday chime. The second twin was equally certain of the origins of his personality style. "The reason is quite simple," he said. "I'm reacting to my mother, who was an absolute slob."

We are, thus, a combination of all of the experiences that bring us to our first meeting with our husband, wife, or intimate partner. Understanding this from an attachment perspective, we—with whatever collection of traits we possess—are seeking connection and psychological safety. A good image of a happy couple who have been together for decades is when one person does something that used to torque the other, but now she just smiles and says, "That's my Jim."

Cathy and Dennis

Even after four months of weekly meetings with Norma, Cathy couldn't help but worry sometimes that Dennis had Asperger's. It felt like she was the one bringing 100 percent of the emotion into their lives. Cathy would feel a constant emptiness she couldn't describe. She had to admit, though, that life felt more stable since they'd started seeing Norma, and that was good. They still had their disagreements. What couple didn't, after all? It wasn't so much *what* they'd disagree about, but how Dennis behaved when they did. He'd go all lawyer on her. He would try to calmly and rationally explain to her why his approach—to Logan or vacations or punctuality or even how much they had sex—was the more reasonable and right one. He had gotten a lot of great insight from Norma about his way of making Cathy feel judged as flawed when they would disagree. She remembers the amazing session they had when Dennis said he *did* think she was smart and capable—he had said he loved that about her—and he had looked at her and said with real feeling, "I love you, Cathy. I want to hear what you have to say. I get worried that my life will fly out of control if I were to be wrong, sometimes." He had even asked her to forgive him. That had just blown her away and they were definitely closer after that. Over the course of time, Dennis would seem more connected, but still he was almost never emotionally expressive, and when she would be upset about something he would always launch into fix-it mode. When they would disagree (even sometimes when they didn't), he would shift almost obsessively into hyper-logic and she'd wonder if there was something wrong with him. She worried if she could be loved the way she needed if Dennis was "on the spectrum," as she and Mary Jane called it.

They had done really good work, in Norma's opinion. Over the period of couples treatment, Cathy had come to understand how her instant anger distressed, even frightened, Dennis. He'd been raised in a non-confrontational family and had never seen his parents fight. With Norma's help, Cathy was able to unpack her reactions when conflict arose with Dennis. The sessions were unexpectedly helpful, and she was glad she and Dennis had not pushed back when Norma told them she needed to see them no less than weekly for a while. Even if they hadn't fought, something would happen during the week that would upset Cathy. Rather than lash out, like before, she would usually withdraw. Things were better, but not yet solid-feeling.

She came to understand that when Dennis was preoccupied or distant, it didn't mean that he was closing off to her. She had slowly come to trust that she was important to him, and she no longer reacted quickly inside with some, "How *dare* he?" message that would come out hot and daggered. For his part, Dennis began to relax, coming to the understanding that Cathy didn't hate him. He had been desperately convinced of that when they had started this work four months before.

Still, she didn't dare talk about her Asperger's fears in front of Dennis. She could choreograph the final, escalating fight in her head, starting with him getting defensive. ("Are you kidding me? I'm a trial lawyer, for God's sake! That is the stupidest thing I've ever heard. If that's how you feel, then we just can't be together.") He might even threaten to take Logan because she would try to interfere with their relationship. He'd no doubt tell her that she was the one who was sick and that she was "borderline." That was like wearing a scarlet "B" on her shirt. Cathy would get stirred up inside and then put the matter to rest. Better to live in peace and not stir the pot.

That changed five months into their therapy.

The fight had started tamely enough. The weather was warming up with spring's appearance, and Dennis had promised he would agree to sleep with the window open when winter was over. Cathy felt claustrophobic with the windows closed at night, but had agreed to this compromise. Dennis wanted to wait another month or two to open them up, though. It was still too cold, he thought. He had gone online and found a couple of articles that described the benefits of sleeping with windows closed (two out of the billion—the others said to keep them open, Cathy was sure). She had compromised and had counted the days until late March. Now he wanted to keep her closed-in and suffocating for another two months. So one night, she blew. She told him she had had it. She couldn't stay married to someone who had no idea about her needs and didn't seem to care. Then she said, "Dennis, there's something wrong with you. I think you're As-perger's." Dennis had stopped all movement and looked at her with the most hurt she had ever seen in another person's face. He then turned on his heels, walked out the front door, slamming it behind him, and left rubber on the driveway as he wheeled onto the street. He didn't come home until two in the morning, smelling uncharacteristi-cally of bourbon and stealthily, so as not to disturb her, getting under the covers. She was still awake, but felt it wiser to pretend she was asleep. The session with Norma was, thankfully, the next day. She finally drifted off to sleep after saying to herself for what seemed like the thousandth time, "Cathy, you've really blown it now." She woke up at eight o'clock with Dennis on top of her, spreading her thighs apart. She let him enter her, and they had furious, eyes-closed sex. Make-up sex had been one of their refuges in the past, and she hoped this was a way to bridge the huge gulf she had detonated between them. Yet, when he was done, he rolled off her, got into the shower, dressed wordlessly, and told her he'd see her at Norma's that night. Then he just walked out the door. At least he didn't slam it this time.

That night, Dennis, who was usually a slow starter in their ses-sions, was the first to speak. "I can't do this anymore. Cathy and I had a disagreement over keeping the bedroom window closed and suddenly she is calling me Asperger's. That is complete bullshit. I am done. I'm done having my character slammed when she is upset. I am *not* Asperger's or defective and I'm goddamn sick of hearing that!" Norma looked at Dennis with concern and said, "Cathy really hit a nerve, didn't she?" "You're goddamn right," said Dennis. (That was two expletives in one minute—very rare for her husband, Cathy noted.) Norma said, "This is important, Dennis. Can you help me understand why this is such a raw place for you?" Dennis took a deep breath and started talking about his early life. They had both talked about their childhood experiences in their work with Norma. It was important to understand their early attachment histories and the lessons they had gleaned about the safety and availability of love and protection in their early lives. Dennis had talked about his years as a loner kid, fascinated with computers and the endless hours of enjoyment he experienced playing computer games online with kids from Newark to Tucson. He had been one of the nerdiest kids in his school, but his 4.0 grades and activities such as all-state miler on the track team and near-concert level skill on the clarinet had gotten him a ticket to Princeton and, later, Cornell Law School. All of this was long-shared background in the therapy with Norma.

However, this night he told a new story. It turns out that when he was twelve, his mother, who carried and dispensed a lot of anxiety in their home, became fixated on a belief that there was something wrong with Dennis. He had but one friend, and Dennis and Jordan communicated almost exclusive by computer. She worried he didn't have friends, and there were so many nice children in the junior orchestra he played in. Dennis once heard his mother and father speaking in heated tones behind their closed bedroom door about him. He remembers being kind of scared to stand by the door and listen. What if the door had flown open and he was standing there? His mother wanted him to be evaluated by a psychiatrist. His father said that was ridiculous. Mom had replied, "How do you know? *You're* not a doctor! You think you are an expert at everything, but you aren't, Donald, and you know it." His father had relented, and Dennis was told the next morning that they wanted him to see a doctor because they were worried he didn't have friends. He had said, "What about

Jordie?" but they both said Jordie wasn't enough. He had been confused, hurt, and resentful, and even Jordan's messaging him, "You're fine, bro," didn't help. The psychiatrist talked to him a couple of times and then had a meeting with his parents. They never told him what was said, but they started giving him new things to do—things he hated. They enrolled him in a dancing class. They signed him up for the youth group in his church. Suddenly he was placed in one awkward group situation after another, and he hated it. He begged his parents to please let him be, and they finally dropped it. He breathed easier. Still, he never shook the feeling that there was something wrong with him—even after setting the school record for the mile in high school, graduating summa from Princeton, and being an editor on the Cornell Law Review. He had loved Cathy's vivacity. He couldn't believe someone as beautiful as her could possibly want to be with him. He had finally been able to put that long-ago doubt about himself to rest. Then Cathy smacked him right between the eyes with it last night.

"So," said Norma, leaning forward in her chair and speaking softly, yet clearly, "no matter how good things may be going with Cathy, there's still this feeling that you'll never be good enough—that you will always be fundamentally flawed in her eyes."

Dennis nodded, tears beginning to brim.

"Could you turn and tell Cathy?" suggested Norma.

Uneasily, Dennis turned to Cathy, who was sharply attentive, and said, "I...wow, this is hard...Cathy, last night—right now, I am so...just, *sad* to think that somewhere, deep down inside, you can never really love and accept me because you believe that I am...I don't know...*missing* something. I have a piece missing, like I'm defective." The brimming tears washed over his eyelids and starting tracing down his cheeks.

Cathy saw the utterly slack, lost feeling on his face as he spoke to her. For the first time in their entire relationship, she understood Dennis's pain around the precise thing she had complained about from what seemed like their first kiss. What came through to her right then was the deep *feeling* Dennis projected. He was about the least autistic-like person she could imagine. Her heart filled with such enveloping care, she reached out to him and asked, "Honey, why hadn't you ever told me this?" He looked up at her, and, without a trace of resentment or defensiveness, in fact with disarming openness, said, "I always felt that there was no way I could make you happy—make you satisfied. You were so angry at me so much of the time and I thought that if I told you about this, you'd think that proved I was defective in some way and you'd leave me. As hard as it all was, I couldn't imagine my life without you—until that week after Gabe's visit made me think I couldn't do it anymore. The last couple of months have been so much better between us. It felt like what you said last night was an ambush. It was like you dropped me off a cliff."

Norma had long known the power of "enactments," which are moments when the dialogue is *between the partners*. Normally, what happens in sessions is that each partner would develop a safe connection with her and she could explore their more sensitive places with them. The connection at that moment would be between her and the individual. While this might prove helpful for the other partner—to hear what may have not been shared in the past—it had nowhere near the power, or bonding potential, as when these feelings, this vulnerability, was shared directly with one's partner. She had seen over the years, in moments too numerous to count, that these moments of transition (from communicating with her to sharing vulnerability and *truth* with their intimate companion) were the most healing elements of her couples work.

That session had felt like a watershed for both of them. Cathy softened in her feelings about Dennis and, while they still operated on different frequencies much of the time, it didn't scare her anymore. She found herself feeling less alone with him. He became marginally more affectionate with her. She started to be able to tell when he needed space and let him be by himself without having her tummy get tied up in a knot. In later sessions, she had been able to share the dark place she feared sliding into when she felt isolated and alone. One night it felt like a dam had burst and her years of feeling frightened and alone gushed out in sobs that lasted fifteen minutes. When she looked up, wary that Dennis would be giving her the old, "What do you want from me?" look, instead she was gazing into moist, compassionate eyes. That was another watershed. It took them a couple more months to consolidate their new gains. Eventually, they were able to joke about some of the things that had driven them both around the bend. Most importantly, they reported to Norma that they were able to talk about previously big trigger topics, like Logan or finances, and when either felt they were moving into high emotional vibration territory, they knew how to take a step back and manage their emotions. Norma was pleased. This work didn't connect with everybody, and she had referred her fair share of couples to a divorce mediator she knew and respected. But it worked way more often than not, and when it did, Norma felt glorious.

OBSERVATION NO. 4
MEN AND WOMEN ARE BOTH FROM EARTH—
BUT THERE ARE DIFFERENCES

Many years ago, John Gray wrote a wildly best-selling book about men being from Mars and women being from Venus. That book stayed in hard cover longer than any other book I can remember. Therapists I have spoken with over the years have been uniformly wary of Gray's blanket statements, yet experts in intimate conflict and its resolution (including John Gottman and Sue Johnson) describe a number of gender differences. I would also say that, *anecdotally*, there are a few broad tendencies that I have seen crop up in the consultation room more often than not.

As a general rule, I've seen women focus more on the relationship and men focus more on autonomy. If the most common dance we see is pursuit and withdrawal, the woman will more likely be the pursuer and the man the withdrawer. This is certainly not a hard-and-fast rule; men can often be pursuers and women withdrawers. Additionally, in same-sex couples, the dance is replicated. As observed by Sue Johnson in *Creating Connection,*[13]

> *The underlying emotional experiences are often different for male and female partners. Female partners more often identify lack of connection and deprivation of contact as the main factor in their distress, whereas male partners more often identify feelings of inadequacy and incompetence as the main element. In similar fashion, emotional distance in relationships has been found to be related to women's*

health status, whereas disagreements and overt averseness have been found to be related to men's health. [14]

Viewed from an attachment perspective, I have seen another dynamic that crops up fairly frequently in the office: Most women in distressed couples are quite high functioning in many areas of their lives. They might have tremendous pain around their intimate relationship, but in business, social interaction, parenting, or all these and more, they are high functioning. When I take even the merest peek into their early lives, the common theme is that they were emotionally on their own. These little girls might have had food on the table and a roof over their head—any observer would see a normal, stable home (for the most part)—but when it came to feeling *seen* and held emotionally when life was fearful or challenging, these girls had to fend for themselves. They didn't wring their hands and bemoan their plight. They carried on. These people learned that there was only one person in the world they could ultimately rely on—themselves. These girls grew up into quite self-sufficient women. Yet, it was self-sufficiency with a confusing twist. There remained a part inside that still longed for that connection—the attachment that told them there was somebody there to catch them if they fell. If life was too much and for a moment they wanted to just collapse, there would be someone there to hold them until they were ready to engage again with their demanding, incredible worlds. At heart, it was the need to be able to depend on another. At the same time, the idea of depending on anyone other than themselves (not just to get certain tasks done, but to let go of the organization and control over life and hand it to another, particularly emotionally) made their skin crawl. This internal battle is waged outside of the presence and awareness of their partner. However, it reflects the greatest of ambivalence (which means being strongly drawn to two opposing places.)

Predictably, these people in their distress will carry on, often with bitterness, about the many ways their partner lets them down and how they would be insane to rely on them. There are often plenty of examples of being disappointed. While there is little doubt that they have been let down at times, the distress and disappointment they reveal in their certainty that, *once again*, they cannot rely on another, is deeply poignant. These people feel alone and don't know how it can be any different in a world that forever lets them down. Of course, if you let your world disappoint you over and over again, to that depth, it sure is going to keep you safe from having to let go and bathe in the experience of being held. That's about as risky as it can get. Helping create a safe environment, where over time this woman's need for care can be explored, is the primary goal. I trained many years ago with a wonderful and wise therapist named John McNeel, and he would often use the phrase, "The sweetness of dependency." He was talking to these people.

Men have presented quite differently in my office, and there is a common theme with many of them that differs from what I have just described. Guys can't show weakness—especially emotional weakness. One of the big goals in relationship work is to help shift people who are intimately bonded from a place of defensiveness and anger to one of connection and safety. It's a *process* and requires patience, but it is a goal many have achieved. One of the steps along the journey occurs when one partner will shift, if just for a moment, from that hard, self-protective space and reach out to the other. The gesture might be a glimpse of vulnerability or a word of tenderness. It is what Gottman calls a "repair attempt." When a couple is clicking, these repair attempts are acknowledged and reciprocated, and the temperature lowers to safe levels. However, one thing I have noticed over time is that men, more than women, tend to respond to the softening from their partner with a continued recitation of old hurts and past insults. I often wonder at this tenacious grip on earlier pains in the face of (what seems, at least, to me to be) ardent attempts by their partner to reach out. I think that what these men are saying is that they still don't believe that their partners fully appreciate the pain they experienced during the fights they've had (and if my partner doesn't understand the raw sharpness of my wounds, how can I believe and trust that they will not strike out again?).

Men are very tender inside but strive mightily to hide it. I've heard men likened to turtles who have a hard shell on the outside but are soft on the inside. Love it or hate it, this is real. Gottman agrees, noting that,

*In 85% of marriages the stonewaller is the husband....
The reason lies in our evolutionary heritage.... To this day,
the male cardiovascular system remains more reactive than
the female and slower to recover from stress. For example,
if a man and woman suddenly hear a very loud, brief sound,
like a blowout, most likely his heart will beat faster than
hers and stay accelerated for longer...*

A man, then, can be so deeply, and *painfully*, triggered by inter-personal distress that he will retreat to safety. The retreat might be actual physical withdrawal, but it can also show up as spacing out and disengagement; obsessive computer use; workaholic behavior; depression; or other ways of building a thick, impregnable protective wall around their tender male hearts.

Emotionally focused couples therapy can be a challenge for guys. Johnson, while extremely warm and filled with compassion, is also a no-nonsense researcher, and when she says that the key to connection for intimate couples is emotion, she's not fooling around. Eventually, if you want to make a transition from conflict and distance to safety and connection, the path is emotion. It's not strategies or homework assignments or communication tools—although all of these have a place and can be helpful. Yet, without emotion, and the vulnerability that accompanies expression of deep emotion, there is no foundation for closeness.

OBSERVATION NO. 5
ANGER ISN'T ALL IT'S CRACKED UP TO BE...
AND IT'S NOT WHAT YOU THINK IT IS, ANYWAY

Viewed from an attachment perspective, anger takes on a different tone and significance in our intimate conflicts. We should start our discussion of anger with the circuits of neurons that course through our brains.

Jaak (pronounced "Yak") Panksepp, a nationally recognized brain researcher, in his studies on the neurobiology of emotion, found anger (or, in his term, "rage") to be one of the seven basic emotional neural circuits.[15] The purpose of fundamental anger is to create boundaries and avoid being boxed into a corner. Mammals use this aggressive emotion if their territory is being invaded (their boundaries violated). A picture depicting anger in Panksepp's book shows a cat, back arched and hissing from a corner.

We all have some personal history with anger and a great number of us were exposed to often frightening levels of this emotion when young. Many associate anger with raised voices, threatening behaviors and punishment. With our natural connection between *conflict* and anger, it is no wonder that we will avoid the former so we don't have to experience the latter.

Small surprise, then, that anger has a personal impact on many therapists, as well. This may be why people who love working with individuals do not like working with couples. While one person may *talk about* anger he has felt or experienced, in an individual therapy session, two people will bring that anger, in all its pulsating power, right into the room with them. A therapist needs to cultivate a certain comfort in the presence of anger. In addition to whatever personal therapy may be helpful in calming the fight-or-flight urges that may surge through us when exposed to expressions of anger, it is necessary to have an *understanding* of anger that permits the professional to work comfortably with people in its throes.

Anger plays a particularly important role in couples therapy. In EFT, therapists refer to "primary anger" as distinct from "secondary anger." Big time *secondary anger* often accompanies a couple to their first meeting with the couples therapist. This secondary anger, which gets our adrenaline surging, feels like a protective shield and is generally understood to cover more vulnerable feelings of sadness or fear or shame. The underlying emotions are usually long-buried and intense, driving the protective anger like the molten lava that flows under an erupting volcano.

The task of the couples therapist is two-fold. First, the secondary anger must be acknowledged as an understandable response to a felt violation. Next, and critically, we must slowly (sometimes *very slowly)* engage in the exploration of the hidden experiences covered by this anger. The greater the shattering of early trust—the deeper the exquisitely painful experience of shame for being exposed as needing and being denied (or mocked or punished for that very need)—the quicker our secondary anger will flash and leap to our protection when interpersonal danger warnings start to flash. For many of us, these alarms are going off constantly, as we have become sensitized to danger in every word or gesture from the people we seek to bring close to us.

If there is one word which may characterize a stable intimate relationship, it is *safety*. Yet, for many of us, since our earliest relationships betrayed our trust and need for a human connection where we felt safe (*i.e.*, a secure *attachment* relationship), we entered adulthood with a craving for this safety *coupled with the certainty that it cannot be found.* No person is safe. Still, the search continues. The need for a secure attachment is hardwired into our brains. We yearn for something which a part of us has decided can never be ours. This certainly will be confirmed in a myriad of great and tiny acts or omissions from our partner. Each moment we are disappointed is absolute, positive *proof* that we cannot trust our partner. The moment from disappointment to shame (for having so exposed our deepest need) to protective rage occurs in a nanosecond. This is secondary anger and we reach its scorching heat in a multi-stage internal process which occurs in a flash.

This is distinguished from "primary anger," which we all need in order to establish and protect our personal boundaries. It doesn't entail volume or personal criticism. Rather, it reflects firmness and clarity. Partners who are able to feel secure with one another can tolerate, even welcome, primary anger. They will hear a clear, firm, expression of anger as an unambiguous message that a line just got crossed and safety needs to be re-established. Since safety is the bottom line goal of securely attached people in intimate relationship, primary anger is welcome information about something very important to our partner.

Interestingly, one of the accomplishments of a couple in Emotionally Focused Couples Therapy is the moment when one partner can use primary anger (*i.e.*, clarity and firmness) to tell the other that their expressions of secondary anger are too painful and need to stop. This can't occur, however, until the partners have established safety between them. Otherwise, it will be heard as a shaming judgment by the anxious and angry partner and the cycle will start spinning again. This may involve weeks (sometimes months) of work to slow down that cycle (which hovers nearby, ready to grab both people and whip them—and Dorothy, Toto, the barn and the cows—into its breakneck spin) and lessen the automatic snap of shame which may easily flood the other, with its accompanying defensiveness or wounding anger. That accomplished, we create a safe space where secondary anger is replaced by reflections of the heartfelt need for connection that all solid attachment relationships satisfy.

Anger, of course, has been an important topic in interpersonal relationships quite apart from its significance in the adult attachment world. Yet, these other discussions almost always address secondary anger and fail to distinguish it from primary anger. In fact, we hold a number of misconceptions about secondary anger, generally. Perhaps the most prevalent is the teakettle analogy—that if you "blow off some steam," you will reduce the internal pressure and feel better. In fact, research has shown that quite the opposite is true. Expression of secondary anger tends to augment the emotion. Express this kind of anger and you are likely to work yourself up and become even more angry.

In her excellent book, *Anger: The Misunderstood Emotion*, Carol Tavris dismisses the "ventilation is good" theory of anger. Tavris cites many studies that, time and again, reach the same conclusion—ventilating anger usually makes you feel worse than before you began spitting venom. As a rule, if you ventilate your anger all over someone, you will like them less afterward, the relationship will be damaged, and you will likely not feel any resolution.

Tavris concludes that there are certain circumstances in which ventilating anger will make you feel better, but the conditions are restrictive. The following five conditions must be met:

First, anger must be directed at the target of your anger.

Second, the expression of anger must restore your sense of control over the situation and your sense of justice.

Third, the expression of anger must change the behavior of the target or give you new insights.

Fourth, you and your target must speak the same anger language.

Fifth, there must be no angry retaliation from your target.

This sounds a lot like rules for the expression of primary anger to me.

Murray Straus, a sociologist in the field of family violence, notes,[16]

> *There is an element of truth in the catharsis notion, but not in the usual idea of physiological relief. If a couple doesn't deal with what is causing their anger, it will remain, or worsen. Unfortunately, most people don't know how to express anger without attacking or belittling.*
>
> *Verbal aggression usually fails because it riles up the other person and makes him or her inclined to strike back, whereas a description of your state of mind constitutes less of an attack, inspiring the other person to make amends. People who shout and yell when they feel angry thus tend not to get the results they hope for (that is, apologies and changed behavior from the yellee), so next time they feel angry they yell louder. The object of their wrath either counterattacks or ignores them.*

As Aristotle noted over 2500 years ago, "Anyone can become angry, that is easy, but to be angry with the right person, to the right degree, at the right time, for the right purpose and in the right way, that is not easy."

OBSERVATION NO. 6
"OVER-CONTROLLING" PEOPLE ARE OFTEN JUST TRYING TO KEEP CHAOS AT BAY

Some complaints are more common than others in a couples therapy consultation room. "She/he is over-controlling" is a frequent complaint. To be sure, constantly being questioned, critiqued, and intervened upon by a partner can feel like you are slowly being squeezed into a tiny, suffocating box. It comes to feel intolerable.

Yet how effective has it been to say, "Back off. You are too controlling"? Most likely you have gotten lots of defensiveness in response. Let's look at this from another perspective.

I want to make it clear that I'm not saying this behavior is fine and you have to learn to live with it. In fact, it's quite the opposite. An important point needs to be made here: A firm bond and strong,

long-term relationship can never be based upon one person deciding
they will live with a situation that makes them deeply unhappy, distant, or self-protective. The goal of all good relationship counseling is
a deeper connection of trust, openness, and love. If anyone feels they
have to "tolerate" certain kinds of unacceptable behavior, they are
buying a ticket on the unhappy train, and they'll need to get off
somewhere down the line.

That said, how do we think about certain kinds of behaviors or
attitudes that drive one partner away from the other? Let's look at the
over-controller, first. All too frequently, a person who needs to direct
their partner's behavior and have things *a certain way* have come
from an early life marked by chaos and uncertainty. It could be as
extreme as alcoholic parents who battled, but it might be as common-
place as being a latchkey kid at an early age because of two working
parents. Without clear adult guidance, and with only himself to establish boundaries and understand what is reasonable and safe, the world
just outside his grasp feels uncontrollable and chaotic. Such people
will often have strong and often harsh judgments of their partners.
There is almost a survival element to the intensity of their hold on
having things *a certain way*.

A word of caution is appropriate, here. There is a difference between the need to control, which is manageable through solid couples
work, and the toxic, destructive power-and-control dynamic of domestic abuse. Indeed, Johnson and others have repeatedly warned that
the vulnerability encouraged by attachment-based therapy is strongly
contra-indicated if domestic violence (broadly defined and not limited to physical abuse) is present. It is absolutely imperative that anyone who struggles with an "over-controlling" partner, particularly
when there is anger on their partner's end, must not rationalize this
behavior through the empathy encouraged in this section. If this is
your situation, you might be in a dangerous domestic prison and you
must share your situation with a professional who is versed in domestic abuse, to assess whether couples therapy can be helpful in your
situation or whether you need support and protection from a psychologically and/or physically dangerous partner.

In situations *not* characterized by domestic abuse, this discussion
is just one example of why solid couples therapy that really connects

people can be deep, rewarding, and often frightening work. The fears that reside inside of us hide in the remote caves of our psyches. We worry that exposing those parts of ourselves is unspeakably risky. So, we do not speak from those places. If we do, we feel certain that we will reveal ourselves as fundamentally weak or defective. That is part of the human condition. We learn who we are in the world at an early age from our families of origin (or their stand-ins). We have known handsome men who secretly felt themselves ugly; brilliant women who privately saw themselves as stupid; competent achievers who deep inside thought themselves losers. Perhaps more frequently, we bury these negative attributes so deeply inside that we have walled them off completely, and they are in another galaxy somewhere within our many billions of neurons—far from awareness and oddly foreign-feeling at the suggestion of their presence. As with so much that is vital inside of us, our adult lives of work, friends, and society do not pinch that sensitive place, so it can stay curled up in the cave, in that nook within the inner recesses of our brains and hearts. That shield dissolves in our adult attachment relationship. That fearful part of ourselves longs to be seen and accepted. It needs to be acknowledged and assured. That seems childish, though, and we're grown-up adults. (In a way, that's the whole point and what ultimately distinguishes our marriage or intimate bond from all other relationships.) In confusion, we act out this iron-fisted need for order, predictability, and security, when the thing we need most is to share our belief that in our inner core the world often seems overwhelming and chaotic...to share this and be assured. Well, right there is the definition of "enormous risk." The more self-assured we have built ourselves to be in our lives, the larger that risk.

We get angry because we can't share with our partner what drives us. How can we share this thing with them, though, if we have been repeatedly criticized for being "over-controlling," maybe even to the point of having a mental disorder? No way. Who do we most need to share this stuff with? Our intimate partner. Who is the least safe person in this dynamic? Our intimate partner. This vital and healing work probably can't be done without the support of an empathic, understanding third person. Most people come to a couples therapist in order to stop fighting. They want tools and schemes and homework.

A roadmap to lead them to a less toxic home life is the principal goal. They will come to see a counselor and after a few sessions might find that things are better and feel they got what they came for and end the work. If this results in a truce but no real sense of closeness or resolution, the chance to find a home in the other's heart will be lost. That, ultimately, is what a securely attached relationship is for all of us, whether infants or adults—to have a home in the other person's heart.

OBSERVATION NO. 7
DEFENSIVENESS IS NATURAL, AUTOMATIC...
AND DESTRUCTIVE

As Sue Johnson has noted, "Angry criticism, viewed through the attachment lens, is most often an attempt to modify the other partner's inaccessibility, and as a protest response to isolation and perceived abandonment by the partner." However, as night follows day, an angry protest, which is experienced as criticism, will naturally and automatically trigger a defensive response. Many, probably most, expressions of anxiety over disconnection begin with the word "you." "You're not as romantic as you used to be." "You always seem so distant." "You care more about your parents than me." "You have an alcohol problem." "When we fight you get abusive." "You have a personality disorder." "You _____."

How are we supposed to respond to these statements that feel like accusations? Almost always, we'll be defensive. You attack. I defend.

Relationship therapist Daniel Wile has described *forty-four* different kinds of defensiveness![17] He breaks these down into six different categories.

Let's take the common scenario suggested by Wile: Bill comes home from a hard and stressful day at work. He kisses his wife, Wendy, and then plops on the couch and turns on the TV for some zone-out time before dinner. Wendy, having had a difficult day herself, feels dismissed, so she goes to Bill and says, "You never talk to me anymore."

Bill's first set of defenses is The Denial, one of Wile's categories. There are four different examples of Denial. The first is *That's not so; what are you talking about?* ("I talk to you all the time.") The second is *Here's evidence.* ("What about Wednesday, when you were upset about your mother and we spent the whole evening talking about it?") The third is *I was just about to do it.* ("I was just on my way to the kitchen to talk to you.") The fourth is *I'm an innocent bystander.* ("What have I done now? I've been sitting here bothering nobody, relaxing after a hard day, just wanting some peace and quiet. What's the big problem?")

These are Wile's other five categories:

- Explaining (Making Excuses), with seven examples
- Counterattacking, with a whopping twenty-five examples
- Self-Accusing, with one example
- Fixing (Rushing Past the Problem to Find a Solution), with four examples
- Withdrawing, with three examples

Despite their wide range and differences in style, they all have one thing in common—they don't respond to the plea from Wendy. Of course, this is understandable, because Bill's automatic response is to protect himself from what feels like an accusation coming from Wendy, with Bill caught in the crosshairs. It's as if Bill, with that metaphorical gun pointed straight at his heart, reacts in immediate self-protective mode. He thinks, "She couldn't *really* be pointing a gun at me right now. I'm seeing things." He says, "Hey, Wendy, look out the window. Isn't that your Aunt Betsy?" "You're crazy. Put that gun down." When she glances out the window, he dives for cover. What do all of these reactions have in common? The only thing Bill is aware of at the moment is the gun and his need to protect himself.

Moving away from the metaphor, how does Wendy feel when Bill responds with any of Wile's forty-four defensive maneuvers? She feels worse—hopeless and unheard. Likely she might begin to feel angry, if she wasn't already. Her next response might be more barbed. The first was a desperate plea to connect, the second more designed to draw blood. Before we know it, Bill, who desperately wants domestic peace and a happy partner, and Wendy, who desperately wants reconnection with her mate, are circling each other in an escalating death-dance. This is why *Defensiveness* is one of Gottman's *Four Horsemen.*

Defensiveness is the antithesis of apology. One extremely common defensive response runs something like this: "I'm *sorry*. Are you satisfied?" The apology we are usually seeking has two important elements. The first is the communication of a real understanding of how one partner's behavior hurt the other person. The second is a deep and honest expression of remorse (because if one cares for this other person, they would not have wanted to hurt them). Many times, the "relationship traumas," as Johnson describes them, were inflicted without thought or knowledge that the other would be hurt deeply. One example occurred in my office recently: The wife had her car in service and she had asked her husband for a lift. He is a very literal and logical thinker, and the first thing that came into his mind was that it was in the opposite direction from where he was going, and he told her it was out of his way and suggested she take the bus. On a 1-10 scale, in terms of his self-absorption and thoughtlessness at the time, where would you put this? It was a one-off experience. Maybe you might place this as high as a 5 or 6? For her, it felt like a 10, and she couldn't shake the feeling of being unloved by him after this. If the discussion were to be about how selfish he was, if he was expected to admit some sort of character defect, he would resist any apology. If the discussion, however, was about her feelings of abandonment at that time and her sudden realization that she wasn't as safe or cared for as she thought she was in this relationship, then we turn from accusation/defense to expression of need and open up the possibility of a caring response.

She could certainly be criticized for coming on so strong and with such anger, but this would be a mistake. We are all highly sensitive to *some* things, and that is what acceptance in relationships is all about. If what she wants is to be seen and loved, telling her that she is over-sensitive (after hurting her) is akin to pouring kerosene on a fire. Again, if the conversation is about how hurt she is, *not* what is wrong with him, he is far less likely to throw judgments her way.

WRAPPING IT ALL UP

In the last two chapters, we've explored one particular, and very effective, way of thinking about couples in conflict. There are other widely accepted approaches for successfully working with couples experiencing stress. One thing these all have in common is that they think of how people react to each other in a different way when locked in intimate conflict. The insights shared here come from viewing intimate relationships as *attachment* bonds. This view is supported by current developments in neuroscience, research into couples therapy conducted by Sue Johnson and others, and scores of examples shared by hundreds of therapists on the EFT email list. Some might find the language here to be overly "touchy-feely," but if there is a world we inhabit that is *all about* deep and vulnerable feelings, it is our intimate relationship. Our friends, business associates, relatives…even our kids don't trigger the basic need we have for security and personal, *emotional* safety in this world.

Maybe these chapters have described a way out of the distress, without having to end the relationship. Maybe they haven't. And maybe it's not yet clear. So, let's take a moment and do a brief inventory to see where we stand.

TAKEAWAYS

- **When an intimate couple is in chronic conflict, it does not help to think of the problem as anyone's fault. (There are certain behaviors, like domestic violence, characterized by power and control dynamics that must stop, or the relationship must end for safety's sake.) The two people are not working together. Their process needs to be identified and repaired. Couples therapy is not a statement of any individual or joint failure.**

- **Think back on your most recent fights. How many of them can be broken down to a cycle of one's criticism and the other's defensiveness? What could you have done differently at that time?**

- **Cut yourself some slack. Intimate conflict is complex and soul-sapping. Get help if you need it.**

CHAPTER 4

The Decision

AT A PERSONAL CROSSROADS

The decision to terminate a committed intimate relationship pretty much *defines* "difficult." Our partner can make it easier by doing something outrageous and obliterating the trust we have in them or our bond. Yet, even then, many of us struggle. The blow of revealed infidelity will not drive everyone away. An attachment bond possesses a special intensity, which might even resist the explosive damage of a sexual or emotional affair.

In such circumstances, as with many others which might be less acute, yet still relationship-deadening, an exploration of the bond and possibilities for repair might be in order. As we observed in the prior section, good couples therapists are *in the business* of supporting the healing and strengthening of the most challenging threats to the bonds of intimacy and trust. These professionals are not unlike the physicians we engage to treat an array of bodily maladies. If we find ourselves short of breath and experiencing chest pain upon the humblest of exertion, we will, no doubt, call up our doctor and get in to her office as fast as we can. We might be referred to a cardiologist, who is *in the business* of treating people with possibly life-threatening heart disease. While they might assess our condition and provide us with suggestions for treatment, if we don't follow their suggestions, well…we'll probably die. Neither the physician nor the couples therapist are miracle workers, but their intervention into our troubles can make all the difference. If we need to drop seventy-five pounds, avoid all summer sun if our skin is sensitive to its rays, or eliminate a much-loved food from our diet, attainment and maintenance of our health can be hard work. Such is the case, as well, if our intimate relationship is burdened by a sudden blow or years of neglect. We might do ourselves a disservice by throwing in the towel simply because the climb is too steep. Yet, as I have said more than once in these pages, trying to fix a damaged relationship on our own will usually lead to frustration and heartache. So, the first step in the process of *deciding* is to get professional help. In the minority of circumstances, where domestic abuse, addiction, or untreated mental illness plague a relationship, that help might be better obtained with an individual counselor. These issues aside, there is much good that can come from a course of couples counseling—even if that good is clarification of the need to end the relationship.

I will admit a bias: I believe that salvageable bonds should be preserved. Too many people pull the plug prematurely, and the pain of dissolution becomes a dear price to pay, usually by both partners.

Yet, I will also admit a softening of my bias over the years. This process was aided by one of my dearest friends, Louis, who married young and had a daughter. His first marriage was unhappy and ended years ago. Later in life, he met his exquisite wife, Loretta, and they have made each other very happy for decades. He is much better for his divorce and remarriage. So, as with just about *everything* in our lives, nuances and complexities abound and there is no hard and fast rule. The need to make this huge transition away from something for which we feel dead inside pushes up against a commensurate desire to maintain stability and the security of the known.

Counseling and psychotherapy have always been a hard sell in this most self-sufficient of societies. Even *admitting* you could be helped by a couples therapist feels like a statement of surrender for some. "We can do this ourselves," is a firm and frequent statement of independence. Sadly, many couples just cannot do it themselves. That doesn't mean you can't *do it*, though; it's just that you may need a coach.

However, what if we have done our work in therapy and are still uncertain? How do we decide? Once the decision is made, how do we know we have chosen well for ourselves?

HOW DO YOU MAKE DECISIONS?

How do you make the biggest decisions in your life?

I'm not talking about the boatload of day-to-day decisions we face every day (pick up the dry-cleaning or the library book first; cook burgers or spaghetti for the kids tonight; comedy or French holocaust documentary on Saturday). I'm talking about the truly *big* decisions with a lot riding on them…like which of two competing, equally attractive job offers to accept, or whether to marry a particular person, or whether to *divorce* a particular person. They are decisions that can have long-term, life-changing consequences. As you might imagine, there are different ways people make the important decisions in their lives.

For a dozen years, I taught law students about the art of counseling clients, which simply boils down to helping them make decisions. I ask the students at the beginning of the discussion how *they* make the important decisions in their lives. The same list goes up on the board year after year:

Count 'Em Up: Draw a line down the middle of a page and put the reasons "pro" on one side and the reasons "con" on the other. The side with the most or best reasons wins.

Ask Mom: Many of us have figures of respect and authority in our lives. Parents, grandparents, godparents, teachers, pastors/imams/rabbis, coaches, or mentors are the most common. (In the 1990s, Hillary Clinton famously communed with Eleanor Roosevelt when she needed advice.) We turn to them for guidance in our times of confusion or challenge.

Pray: Many of us receive peace and profound guidance through prayer. Prayer may serve as a window to your own wisdom or provide a transcendent message from a higher, loving power. Millions of us find the calm certitude and direction we earnestly seek through prayer.

Hash It Out With Your Best Friend: We might not be looking for someone to tell us what to do so much as having a sounding board that lets us talk it out ourselves and find our own answer. Sure, there might be a healthy dollop of advice thrown in, too, but this is basically a self-generated answer process.

Listen to Your Gut: Perhaps one of the most comforting and unnerving messages in the self-help world is, "The answer lies within you." That's good, because the answer is very likely to be *your* answer for yourself, which will be closer to the bull's-eye for your unique needs. That's not so good when you can't divine the answer that's presumably lying right inside you, waiting to be found. Luckily, there are tried and true approaches to learning how to relax, utterly, and see what inner wisdom arises. (Two approaches I like quite a bit are Focusing, developed by Eugene Gendlin, and the guided imagery of Martin Rossman, which can be downloaded from his www. worrysolution.com website.)

Let the Decision Come to You: Many people find that if they do nothing, the decision will basically make itself. Life is hardly ever static. We can stand still and do nothing and the world will still swirl around us. Eventually circumstances will pile up on one side or the other, and we will be forced to go with that particular flow, in that particular direction—whether it's the right direction for us or not…but at least the decision will be made!

We can use any one of these or a combination. Whichever method is employed, there are a couple of more things to understand about decisions.

A BRIEF PEEK UNDER THE HOOD
~ TWO BASIC DECISION-MAKING STYLES ~

For some of us, decisions aren't that hard. In fact *not* making a decision is like torture. There are those who by temperament need to make a decision and have the ambiguity settled. They are known in the world of Myers-Briggs Psychological Types as "Judgers." One character trait that stands out for these folks is their quickness in making a call and moving on.

For those among us who tend in the opposite direction, we are known as "Perceivers" in Myers-Briggs parlance. When faced with a decision, Perceivers tend to perseverate, seeing clearly the pros and cons of any side of a decision and hoping one more bit of information can come along that will make the best path clearer. We can wait and wait......and wait. Sadly, it will seldom become easier with more information and more time. While ambiguity makes the Judger grit her teeth, the act of deciding does the exact same thing for the Perceiver. Each character brings with it benefits and challenges. The Judger can make a decision and not look back—but the risk is that the *need* to have things decided will push her to a premature decision before all the necessary information is in. The Perceiver is open about taking in necessary information, but the over-concern about getting it wrong will push the decision off further and further.

Decisions unmade keep us mired in unfulfilling and desperate lives. We feel stuck and our life energy is diverted inwardly. Take the decision that drives this section: whether to leave an intimate relationship that is causing pain and distressing preoccupation or to stay and work together to create what you need. Either way we go requires deep commitment. That commitment is impossible unless you have made the decision.

While there might be no more wrenching decision than The Divorce Decision, it is still a far more acceptable choice in the current era. Social stigma directed toward divorce has waned in the past decades so as to be invisible.[18] Marriage for romantic love has dominated our thinking since the Victorian era. "I love him but I'm not *in love with* him," is a common enough refrain. Changing partners has been compared to changing a suit of clothes. Yet we know that the emotional devastation that might follow this life transition for many of us renders it all quite a bit more complicated than that.

GETTING OUT

While the calculus of leaving a relationship can be quite complex, there are some clear indicators that a marriage is unsustainable. Domestic abuse characterized by power and control dynamics is a dark prison—frightening and dangerous. Extricating oneself from such a situation is treacherous and requires courage and professional support. However, this must be accomplished. An intimate relationship burdened by untreated substance abuse forces all of our psychic energy into dealing with the hold of addiction. The same can be said for untreated mental disorders that divert attention constantly from the task of recognizing, nurturing, and deepening the attachment bond, which is the relationship's true gift. Care must be taken in addressing these challenges because the risk of labeling and defensiveness is so high. A person's struggle with alcohol or a personality disorder is not the "problem" that is wrecking the relationship. If framed that way, nobody will accept their own struggle and move toward health. ("I will *not* admit my alcoholism, if to do so will only prove my partner was right all along and *I* was the problem in our relationship.") Just as one person must seek treatment and personal healing, the other must shift their lens from blame and frustration to compassion—yet always remain tied to the realization that they cannot continue to exist in a world burdened by untreated addiction or mental illness.

Infidelity is a massive blow to the security of an intimate relationship. Divorce lawyers almost casually refer to the affair as the reason for the split, naturally concluding that a direct line leads inexorably from infidelity to divorce. Yet, ask a couples therapist and a different message will emerge.

Thousands of marital therapists throughout the U.S. have successfully supported a couple's healing from this admitted relationship trauma. It is *not* inevitable that the discovered affair will be the nuclear detonation that annihilates the relationship. However, the process of forgiveness, rebalancing and even deepening the bond is hard, hard work for each partner. If neither is up for the challenge, then this book should be gently closed, given to a friend and the first volume, *Divorce,* should be opened.

Successful navigation through these turbulent times depends on many factors, including the bond's strength in the past; the transgressor's true remorse and willingness to do what is needed to provide the transparency necessary to reassure their partner; the betrayed partner's emotional vulnerability; the couple's social and therapeutic support; and their commitment to their relationship. Unquestionably, if the transgressor is unwilling to completely terminate contact with the affair partner, pick up *Divorce*. If the betrayed partner holds onto the affair as proof of the other's perfidy, extending to before the affair's discovery and uses it as a cudgel to brain the remorseful transgressor over and over, they should either do some serious personal therapy to see if they can trust this person ever again...or just pick up *Divorce*.

Sexual addiction is a real thing and reflects an intense drive to fill an unfillable hole (at least by *that*). Discovered infidelity may be the tip of that particular iceberg. Still, the intimate bond can withstand such a blow, if both partners are willing to roll up their sleeves and do the work which is required. Sexual addiction requires more than smirks and winks. It is a compulsive behavior that can drive a person to lose much more than the shallow gains of a new, exciting experience. Work should begin with a Nationally Certified Sex Addiction Therapist (CSAT). An excellent description of this affliction and its impact on the sufferer and their partner can be found in Dr. Patrick Carnes' *Out of the Shadows: Understanding Sexual Addiction.*

Two additional books, which are entirely devoted to recovery from infidelity are *NOT "Just Friends": Rebuilding Trust and Recovering Your Sanity After Infidelity,* by Shirley Glass and Jean Staeheli, and *After the Affair: Healing the Pain and Rebuilding Trust When a Partner Has Been Unfaithful,* by Janis Abrahms Spring.

The shattering of trust that occurs with infidelity may render these intimate wounds unhealable. Usually, this will occur after years of conflict and distancing—a general erosion of the tie that binds two people to one another. Over time, one-by-one, the fibers of the cable that connects you will snap until the fundamental emotional connection is severed. One person is simply *done*. Yet we may remain, to the consternation of those who love and support us and that inner voice that we are ignoring.

Fear of the unknown can blind us to the obvious path lying before us. That fork in the road is a mirage. We know what to do but deny this fact. Too many other considerations crowd our thinking. Will I be alone for the rest of my life? What about the kids? Am I going to end up on the street? What will my family or my community say? These babbling voices in our heads need to be dialed *way* down and the only two questions left should be:

- Can I build, or restore, a safe, vital, intimate relationship with this person?

- Do I want to?

If you cannot answer both of these questions in the affirmative, you are living within a dry, life-sapping shell. Come to think of it, there is *one more* question you need to ask yourself: Do I want to live within a dry, life-sapping shell? It's not a frivolous question. If your answer to that is "No" as well, then you may want to pick up a copy of *Divorce*.

These fundamental blockages aside, how is one to know if they must move to sever the bonds of an intimate relationship? It can't be based on the myth that divorce is easy, because that's just not true. It also shouldn't be based on the mistaken belief that a marriage cannot withstand basic differences between the partners. Even pain that has continued for years is not a reason to believe that this *thing* you have created with someone else must terminate. I repeat my recommendation to seek professional support. At the very least, you can gain clarity about your decision and, most importantly, receive help in approaching this massive life transition with strength and compassion. You will need boatloads of both.

Still, remaining in an intimate relationship which has died for you is fundamentally life-denying. You might have married at a young age, when you were both partly formed adults, and this person is hardly a friend or companion any more. It is possible to grow apart, and it feels like nothing is left for you here. How will you know if it is time to cut the bond?

A question I often ask people who are struggling with the decision is, "If by some miracle, the conflict or pain of disconnection or mistrust could end in this relationship, and you could have a close, loving bond *with this person*, would you want that?" I have been amazed, at times, with the speed of the answer, "Absolutely," by some. This has been uttered after a clear statement of the pain and vast emotional distance that currently exists and the intolerability of continuing. Others pause, some for…a…long…time before they say, "I don't know." I usually press them gently to pursue the question a bit more deeply, and the response is usually a conflicted and quiet, "No." The conflict is, of course, quite understandable, because few decisions to end an intimate relationship come without inner conflict.

There is guilt. There is worry that this important decision will turn out to be a mistake—whichever side we fall on. Yet, the ambivalence in the answer is not necessarily a reflection of the wisdom of the decision.

A MOST *PERSONAL* DECISION

We can go back and remind ourselves of the many different ways we make a decision in our lives. Ultimately, we must recall that it is *our* decision in *our* lives, and while others might care for us deeply and be generous with advice, they will not have to live with the outcome. We will. So, it is best to listen to our own wisdom. Nobody knows us better than we do, ourselves. If we struggle with a lack of trust in our own decision-making, or if our decisions are forced upon us by crises, then it is best to seek support from someone who can help us discover what is best for ourselves and manage the often painful life challenges that might naturally follow.

There will seldom, if ever, be an explosive moment where the good marriage becomes bad. As Pepper Schwartz, a noted relationship expert, has observed, "Some relationships have been in decline for decades and finally lose all their juice. A marriage doesn't usually just blow up. It's more like a balloon that has been seeping air for a long time. After a while, it's totally deflated."

Good people—people of integrity—make the decision to end their marriages every hour. The individual will look deep inside and cannot say "Yes" to whether they would desire a close, non-conflicted connection with that other person, because they are just, simply, *done*. They have bounced up against that divorce wall a number of times and suddenly one day, they just pass through it and cannot return to the other side. It's sad and it's scary, but that's the truth. That is *their* truth. For those who, sadly, have concluded that they cannot remain in a marriage, the real question is no longer "whether," but "how?" How can a person manage the divorce transition in the healthiest, least destructive manner?

These are complex questions and I invite you to open the first book in this set to gain a clearer understanding of the psychological, emotional and legal challenges which you must address to divorce well.

STAYING IN

Maybe I haven't said this yet, but: If you want to heal a damaged and struggling intimate relationship, *you will need help.* Most couples just can't do it on their own. The environment of the relationship has just become too hot or too cold. Either way, it is definitely too unsafe. We need to be safe to show the parts of ourselves we shield from everybody else. We need to be safe to explore and express our sexuality. We need to be safe to let someone else know about the places where we can be hurt by them and know that they will always take care. Mistakes may be made, but honest repair efforts follow.

We need a safe haven, a secure base and the consistent closeness of another. Couples in distress have already gone through a number of stages together and have a history. Each has let the other one at least partially in. Also, almost every strong adult attachment bond has gone through one or more periods of great challenge in its history. If you are in the middle of yours, this does not mean you must dissolve your bond.

The careful balance we undertake inside ourselves is maddening. "Am I in or am I out?" Either choice requires commitment, good will and loads of integrity. Either choice requires courage. I wish all these things for you.

In reviewing these pages one final time before sending them off in final form, I see that I am an optimist at heart. I am inclined to give people the benefit of the doubt and view certain narrow, self-serving, and harmful behaviors as emanations of a fearful and uncertain heart, rather than venality and ill will. This is clearly not the book of a cynic. In saying this, I want to acknowledge the viewpoint of the cynics, who would say that the actions and outcomes I describe here are unrealistic, the product of a naïve attitude that might render us dangerously vulnerable to the malevolent or manipulative actor. I concede that this risk exists. Yet, I also ask, "What choice do we have, if we want to move toward outcomes that reflect our highest, best selves?" Indeed, this book could just as well be titled *Vulnerability*, because this is the key to connection and mutually satisfactory outcomes (when the heart is involved). If vulnerability would be truly unsafe, then these approaches are not practical. So we must balance our natural inclination toward self-protection with a commensurate commitment to openness when struggling with *intimate conflict.*

I have often joked to workshop participants that almost every question to a lawyer will evoke the same two-word answer. I ask if they know what that is. After a moment of silence, usually someone calls it out: *It depends.*

I also have a two-word description of everything I have spoken of in these pages—the struggles of intimate partners to find balance and reconnection and the decision by one partner to end the relationship,: *It's complicated.*

Yet complication never means absence of a solution. I hope that in these pages, I have introduced you to the powerful and productive ways that committed *service* professionals are thinking about age-old problems.

We live in a fearful age. Change is wickedly rapid, shifting the foundation underneath us whenever we feel we have gained secure purchase. As a lover of history, I can say with certainty that this has been the experience of every generation in this vital, energetic society since John Hancock designed that insurance company logo, though with every generation the speed of change vaults another few notches. Technology and interconnectedness, rapid shifts in mores, and new threats to our security, all put us in a state of near constant anxiety. When fear runs through all of our lives, like a deep background vibration, seldom heard but constantly felt, we will *always* have a tendency to grab onto polarized positions. The greater our fear, the more difficult it is to accept ambiguity. Yet ambiguity...*complexity*...is the reality of our lives.

When our closest, most intimate, relationship is in crisis, that background *thrummm* of fear and anxiety moves to the front of our awareness. Our tendency will always be, in some degree or another, to protect ourselves and those children we hold so dear. Without a path that we can see to get from here to there, we will *always* experience heightened anxiety. With that comes fear, and with that comes polarization and intolerance of ambiguity. There is the desperate, understandable attempt to make the complex simple. But the complex cannot be made simple. It can be explained. It can be broken down into manageable steps. It can be faced with the help of experienced, compassionate guides.

Within the complexity of our lives and those attachment bonds that run deeply and intensely inside of us comes our greatest challenge and truest peace. With the greatest respect and fondness, I hope that these pages have provided some insight, a degree of guidance, and some avenues for experiencing the truest embrace of self-care.

A NOTE OF GRATITUDE

Everything starts and ends with my own beloved, Beverly. You are my secure base, my safe haven, my rock and my warm sunshine. If you laughed at any of my stupid jokes, you'd be perfect.

To my brilliant chums who gave me exceptional feedback and guidance: Bev, Francine Gaillour, Tonia Sassi, Stevan Bosanac, Erin Marquardt, Victoria Livingston, Paul David, Stephen Faulstich, Mike Fancher, Don Desonier, Robert Ritchie, Neil Selman, Brad Lancaster and Steve Gaddis. Your contributions warmed my heart and filled my brain. Thank you Karen Bonnell for your constant encouragement. To Neil, thank you for the greatest sentence in all of literature.

To Jennifer D. Munro, who edited the first edition of this manuscript with great care. Your work taught me more about writing than I could ever have imagined and I am eternally grateful for your kindness and intellect. Thanks for laughing at my jokes!

Thank you, Leonard Shaw, for your supportive words when I struggled with *whether* to do this. Your love is really quite boundless. Also to the other therapists and mentors who have touched me over the years: Jan Lustig, John McNeel, Peg Blackstone, Mary Blackburn, Ellen Ostrow, and Bill Cooper.

To my EFT pals who are so full of compassion and intelligence.

And finally to my clients over the years, both legal and therapeutic. Allowing me to join with you in your journeys has always been, and remains, the greatest privilege of my life, which I will treasure always.

ENDNOTES

[1] These include, of course, Sue Johnson, as well as my own trainers Yolanda von Hockauf, Veronica Kallos-Lilly and Roy Hodgson. Other prominent names include Gail Palmer, Brent Bradley, Scott Wooley, Lorrie Brubacher, George Faller, Jim Furrow, Rebecca Jorgenson and Jim Thomas. See the ICEEFT website for other masters in the field.

[2] Gottmans's book, *The Seven Principles for Making Marriage Work* (2000), is a treasure trove of insight and practical advice. I share Gottman's 69% rule with just about every couple that comes to my office. His observations about males' physiological response to conflict; the three different, and effective, conflict styles of couples; the need for the woman in relationships to engage in a "soft start-up" when voicing a complaint (with examples of how to do this); the need for the male to let his spouse influence him and the corrosive force of his failing to do so; the importance of "repair attempts" after conflict; and the necessity of responding positively to these are just a handful of the many fascinating insights shared in this book. Without question, this is one of my top five favorite books about intimate bonds, the threats that beset them, and methods to protect them. Highly recommended.

[3] Good therapy may be seen as a balance between psychological archeology and attendance to the present. It is important to understand where we are in the context of our lives—what experiences helped shape us. Yet, we can become lost in the past, perhaps in search of that magic core answer to our distress, and in the process lose sight of what is happening right now. EFT attends to a great degree on what is happening inside of each person *now*, in the room. These two forces—the impact of our life course and our current experience need to be balanced.

[4] Roger Fisher, William Ury and Bruce Patton, *Getting to Yes: Negotiating Agreement Without Giving In* (1991) was originally published by Fisher and Ury in 1981. It was immediately recognized as a classic shift in thinking about managing conflict and remains an admired and important cornerstone in the foundational literature on negotiation and conflict. It is short, accessible, and, together with Patton's later book written with Douglas Stone, *Difficult Conversations, How to Discuss What Matters Most (2010),* forms part of this one-two punch of books that will change your thinking about your own conflicts in profound ways.

[5] This very descriptive term was coined by Kate Scharff, MSW, and Lisa Herrick, PhD in their ABA-Published book *Navigating Emotional Currents in Collaborative Divorce: A Guide to Enlightened Team Practice (2011).* In 2011, I attended a workshop at the annual IACP Conference in San Francisco, run by Kate and Lisa and a couple of colleagues from the Washington

D.C. area. It was there I was introduced to their concept of "lock and key," which is a nice way of describing an old systems concept of "complementary functioning" of people in relationship. They describe this in greater detail in their book. At their presentation, I was entranced by Lisa and Kate's compassionate responses to the pain and conflict flowing through divorcing individuals. What was *particularly* impactful for me was the openness they displayed with one another. They modelled a process in which professionals step away from the personas they believe they must maintain and proceed to share their doubts, vulnerabilities, and sensitive spots with one another. Since that demonstration, I have been convinced—and worked to convince my colleagues in the Northwest—that a truly effective team is composed of human beings who show themselves to one another, who respect one another, and who accept one another......and then roll up their sleeves *as a team* and help the struggling family they have joined in the process.

[6] Mary Main of U.C. Berkeley and Peter Fonagy from Great Britain are the two most respected, early explicators of adult attachment styles. Main developed a widely used instrument called the Adult Attachment Interview, which affords a clear window into one's adult attachment style. The interview is *very formal and structured.* Practitioners are intensively trained so they can ask the exact same questions, word for word, in the same way with all interviewees. Not only is the *content* of the responses important, but also the manner of response—length, emotionality displayed, ability to stay on topic—just a wide variety of factors are taken into consideration. Main and Fonagy are often considered the direct descendants of Bowlby and Ainsworth. (Bowlby, Ainsworth and Main flow like Abraham, Isaac and Jacob.) Their contributions are thoroughly described in Karen's *Becoming Attached.*

[7] Eckman's *Emotions Revealed: Recognizing Faces and Feelings to Improve Communication and Emotional Life* (2003) is a masterful compendium, filled with pictures of scores of faces—some posed in studios, some from news photos, others of Papua New Guineans—displaying the characteristic expressions of the basic emotions referenced in the text. Disgust, for example, is characterized, in part, by an upturning of the upper lip. It might be instantly present, then gone, but it is a telltale sign. Part of Gottman's research is to slow down the video recordings of intimate partners engaged in conflict. At a workshop, I recall him pointing excitedly at the briefest of expressions of disgust that might be entirely missed at normal speed. The turn of our mouths, widening or narrowing of our eyes, flaring of nostrils—the 25 facial muscles not devoted to chewing are engaged in the expression of emo-

tion. Eckman's most well-known efforts in recent years have turned to un-covering lies through facial expression.

[8] Antonio Damasio, *Descartes' Error (2005).* Philosopher Rene Descartes famously said, "I think, therefore I am." Damasio found this statement to be in error (thus the title of his influential book). A cornerstone of the theory espoused by this neuroscientist is that feelings are indispensable to the deci-sion-making process and are central to our ordering and values.

[9] Theodore Millon and Carrie Millon, *Personality Disorders in Modern Life* (2000). Millon's work is highly readable and full of insight. One of his greatest contributions, in my view, is that he describes personality disorders not as some discrete illness, like polio or the flu, but a spot on a continuum. The characteristics of individuals with the extreme "locked in" experience of a personality disorder have personality characteristics which are found, in less extreme degree, in people who are successful, well-adjusted adults.

[10] The ideas about the personality characteristics lying on the extreme oppo-site end of the extreme pendular swing of a personality disorder are mine and may be disputed by other therapists. I have found it to be a very helpful or-ganizing principle.

[11] Dan Wile, *After the Honeymoon (2008).*

[12] Robert Karen, PhD, *Becoming Attached: First Relationships and How They Shape Our Capacity to Love* (1994). This is, unquestionably, one of my top five favorite books (and when you consider that one of the Hardy Boys books is on the list, this covers a lot of ground!). Karen combines a wonder-ful, descriptive writing style with his professional interests and knowledge and the benefit of having spent hours interviewing many of the major players in the decades-long story of attachment. The book tells a fascinating tale of the social currents that both supported and buffeted attachment throughout the years. For example, Karen discusses the reaction of the rising tide of mothers who chose, or needed, to return to the workforce and pursue careers (seeking the same rewards as men had long enjoyed from these efforts) and had to respond to the claims that being away from their children all day was depriving them of a primary attachment figure, thereby destroying their psy-ches and lives. (How's *that* for a burden?) The following discussion of other consistently present, caring adults as adequate attachment figures addressed the preceding story of conflict. This is but one of the many fascinating, beau-tifully written dramas that have characterized the establishment of attach-ment as a dominant theory of personal development, mental health, and rela-tionship stability and satisfaction.

[13] *Creating Connection* is directed to therapists. For two excellent discussions by Johnson for non-professionals, see *Love Sense (2014)* and *Hold Me Tight* (2008). The latter has been a mainstay recommendation by almost every emotionally focused couples therapist I know. Johnson describes many examples of conflict and the cycle, some of which are almost guaranteed to get a "Hey, that's us!" reaction from readers.

[14] Johnson, *Creating Connection: The Practice of Emotionally Focused Couple Therapy* (2004). This is the book that introduced me to EFT, read in preparation for the transformative four-day training with Sue Johnson. I highly recommend this book to any person who is interested in working professionally with struggling intimate couples—be it therapists or family lawyers. Johnson melds systems thinking and attachment in a seamless and compelling fashion. The book also lays out the *theoretical* basis for EFT and describes its progressive steps. This is *not* an approach to couples therapy that is seat-of-your-pants in nature (although each session will have its fair share of moment by moment challenges that require appropriate response—which can feel to some like sliding down an ice sheet by...the seat of your pants). EFT, as set forth in this work, displays careful thought and a clear "roadmap" for the therapist. This roadmap is summarized in the Appendix.

[15] Along with Searching, Lust, Play, Attachment, Nurturance and Fear. See, Jaak Pankseep, *Affective Neuroscience, The Foundations of Human and Animal Emotions* (1998).

[16] Carol Tavris, *Anger – The Misunderstood Emotion* (1982). This is a masterful tome, filled with wit and insight. To understand anger, embrace its presence and functions, and to express it wisely and productively are the key messages of this book. Tavris is an insightful observer of our cultural emotional predilections, with a more current book, *Mistakes Were Made (but not by me)* standing as an excellent discussion of rationalization of destructive, cruel, or thoughtless behavior. This one is also highly recommended.

[17] Dan Wile, *After the Fight: Using Your Disagreements to Build a Stronger Relationship* (1995). I can easily say that the one-day Wile workshop I attended years ago comes a close second behind Gottman's masterful presentation I referenced in the text. You really cannot help but like the guy. There is great similarity between Wile's approach and Johnson's. The major difference, I believe, was in Wile's practice of standing (or kneeling) beside one partner and expressing their need in a more palatable and empathic manner, while Johnson's method supports the partners in coming up with their own language and finding a way to do this themselves. Be that as it may, I thoroughly enjoyed this book and recommend it to any therapist who works with couples.

---

[18] Stephanie Coontz, *Marriage, a History: How Love Conquered Marriage* (2005). The blurb printed on the front cover of my paperback edition is from the *Oprah* magazine and says, "Myth-shattering. Endlessly fascinating." C'mon! If Oprah likes the book, what more need be said? Stephanie Coontz *is* an excellent writer. This enjoyable and informative book is obviously the product of years of intensive research by Coontz. Her portrait of marriage in the Middle Ages (the differences between royal marriage and that of the peasantry); the way Victorian England forever changed our view of marriage; and the modern social forces heaving against the institution are but a handful of discussions that make this book…well, endlessly fascinating.

APPENDIX

BOOKS

Everybody's got their favorite books. Here are some of mine. The works listed below are simply the ones that have impacted me over the years. Much of my thinking germinated from the seeds planted by these authors, but by no means are these books the best or only things written about relationships, divorce, attachment or just simply taking care of yourself. The few works of fiction, greater number of mysteries, and even greater number of histories, and other assorted non-fiction which have taken up the lion's share of my lying-by-the-fire reading only influenced this book in an indirect way, difficult to discern and describe. However, here are the top books that influenced this one and if you are going to do any further reading, these are the ones recommended:

Becoming Attached – First Relationships and How They Shape Our Capacity to Love, by Robert Karen: No surprise this is the book at the top. It ranks as one of the best book of any kind I have ever read. Karen is a psychologist and extraordinary writer. The story of the development of attachment theory is really edge-of-your-seat dramatic in places and his descriptions of the stellar lights of the field, like John Bowlby and Mary Ainsworth are beautifully wrought and deeply humanizing. Attachment, in addition to being a powerful description of how we are the way we are, is also a riveting social/political story as well. The blowback from women in the 70's and 80's, who were entering the workforce and claiming careers, only to be told that their time away from their babies was ruining them for life, is just one example. A beautiful book, exquisitely rendered.

The Seven Principles for Making Marriage Work, by John Gottman, Ph.D. and Nan Silver: That mesmerizing weekend in Portland many years ago, in which Gottman sat before a couple hundred therapists, alone with his Powerpoint and keen intelligence, is almost completely encapsulated in this slender, very readable volume. For my money, this is the best "how to" couples self-help book on the market. As he makes very clear, conflict is *not* the problem in intimate relationships. It is whether the people permit the conflict to surge and over-run their connection, bringing a host of avoidable destructive forces like his Four Horsemen; depletion of the "emotional bank account;" failure of the male to allow his partner to influence him and the equally damaging failure of his partner to understand the need for the "softened start-up" when raising complaints. While the actual *practice* of Emotionally Focused Therapy seems to me to be a preferable clinical approach, the "psychoeducation" provided by

Gottman and his years of research into couples' conflict is indispensable. It comprises a significant part of my work with couples who are periodically regaled with another Gottman tidbit.

Getting to Yes by Roger Fisher, William Ury and Bruce Patton: There are so many books about mediation out there, any reasonable bibliography on the subject would go on for pages. However no work better demystifies conflict than this true classic in the dispute resolution literature. Unlike so many other excellent books about mediation of disputes, this is written for Regular Joe and Joan's. It is compact and can be easily devoured in one or two sittings. There isn't a mediator worth his or her salt who doesn't incorporate the fundamental elements of *Getting to Yes* in their practice. These authors, and their progeny in the Harvard Negotiation Project, have written other extremely valuable works like Ury's *Getting Past No* and the truly excellent (and a whisker away from being on the list at this spot, *Difficult Conversations* by Douglas Stone and Sheela Heen…Oh what the heck! Make this one a "two-fer" and read that one too. These two books will utterly *transform* the way you think about, and manage, all conflicts in your life – whether it is at home or at work.

Hold Me Tight – Seven Conversations for a Lifetime of Love, by Susan Johnson: This is the Classic. There's no other way to say it. Sue Johnson managed, in this very accessible volume, to explain what adult attachment is and how it rattles our cages (and our bones). Nothing throws us more off-balance than the anxiety that is sparked and fueled by intimate conflict. No book explains this more clearly, eloquently and compassionately than this. The Emotionally Focused Therapy community throughout the world devours the training DVD's prepared by Johnson and she is spoken of in deservedly reverential tones. This little woman is a giant, in that she has been able to combine an exacting academic intelligence with almost Buddha-like compassion for the struggling couples she touches. I have preferred her professional training materials like The Practice of Emotionally Focused Couples Therapy and Emotionally Focused Couple Therapy With Trauma Survivors. However, there is no better description of this marvelous, creative work for the lay public than *Hold Me Tight*.

Type Talk – The 16 Personality Types That Determine How We Live, Love and Work by Otto Kroeger and Janet Thuesen: I'd say that no better introduction to psychological type may be had. Over the last few decades, certain individuals and teams have arisen across the nation to provide training and instruction in Myers-Briggs Type, but these people have been the gold standard. This volume (and their follow-up, *Type Talk at Work)* are so clear, so accessible and so full of salient examples that readers will not be able to set it down without having learned valuable lessons about what makes them (and others) tick. In reviewing my old dog-eared volume for this book, I found scores of comments highlighted, with corresponding notes "Me" or "Suzie" or "Mark." Little bits and pieces just *perfectly* described various people in my life at the time – and since. Take it from this INFP, this is the one to get.

After the Fight – Using Your Disagreements to Build a Stronger Relationship, by Daniel Wile: Nobody wrestles with the challenges of couples therapy with quite this mix of compassion, experience and humor. Wile knows whereof he speaks, being an extremely seasoned couples therapist. His work is actually quite similar to Johnson's, but he contributes his own special voice to the conversation. Nobody is so good at giving us the hard news that *every* close relationship is at times infuriating, annoying and discouraging – but with the corresponding message that, "It's all okay. You'll be fine." Perhaps no one is as good at describing the incredibly sensitive spots that get rubbed, *hard*, during intimate conflict and the automatic reactions we all experience as we try to protect ourselves. Read in tandem with Johnson, we come to understand why intimate conflicts affects us so, and why they are so difficult.

Take Back Your Marriage by William Doherty: Bill Doherty just may be the dean of American couples therapists. A long-time head of the marital therapy department at University of Minnesota, he gave us this thin, yet surprisingly profound volume some years ago. There are two strong themes to this book. The first is that we are hobbled in this age by what he calls a "consumer approach" to marriage. How easy it is for us to feel, at the strong twinges of dissatisfaction, that we can do better. We will discard this model and go for a newer, better one. Doherty explores this mindset with a critical and dismayed eye. With many examples, he describes how easy it has become to just move on. The second, lengthier, part of the book talks about what brings couples to this state. He compares marriage to a boat on the Mississippi River just outside his office window. The current is not fast, but it is unrelenting, and if you don't paddle at all, you'll find yourself far downstream and far away from where you had wanted. As with a boat on the Mississippi, a marriage can find itself being slowly, inexorably swept over the falls by so many demands on our time and attention. Surely children will take us away from each other…as will work, socializing, computers and a host of other demands or interests. Thus, Doherty introduces us to the notion of rituals of connection, which, if attended to, can inoculate a relationship form those forces that will pull us apart. An excellent volume.

An EFT Roadmap for Couples

Reprinted by permission from :

Pat LaDouceur, Ph.D., L.M.F.T. Berkeley, California
Veronica Kallos-Lilly, Ph.D., R.Psych., Vancouver, B.C.

Sometimes the couples we see wonder, "where they are" in the therapy process. I (Pat) wanted to create something related to Hold Me Tight that would help them see their gains, understand the rough spots, and know what to look forward to. The following is a suggested approach.

Stage 1 – Understand Your Strengths and the Patterns that Keep You Stuck

Step 1: Set goals for counseling; understand some of the ways your relationship history affects your relationship now.

Step 2: Discover and describe the negative patterns of interaction you get stuck in. You and your therapist will track your interactions with your partner and identify where and how your communication breaks down.

Step 3: Emotions are stirred up in your relationship, especially when you get stuck in these negative cycles of interaction. Emotions also drive the cycle. You may first be aware of anger, frustration, anxiety, numbness or even withdrawal. Notice inside what other feelings are beneath these initial feelings, such as hurt, sadness or fear. Begin to share these "underneath" feelings with your partner. It is OK if it feels "bumpy" – it helps diffuse the cycle sometimes, but not always.

Step 4: Describe your cycle and recognize what the triggers are. Understand how the things that you do to protect yourself and your relationship affect and may even threaten your partner. Notice how you co-create the cycle: "we're doing that thing again...the more I go after you, the more you withdraw because you're feeling hurt..." Slow down your conversations so that you can tap into the feelings that are beneath the surface. Catch your own thoughts (e.g., "She doesn't care" or "I don't matter") before acting on them. You might notice that you can hold back your knee jerk reactions to avoid the cycle. You might not know yet how to pull each other close and you might be afraid the "old way" will come back. However, when you discover that this negative cycle is the source of unhappiness in your relationship, you realize that your partner is not the enemy. You can then work together to gain control over this negative cycle and that already feels infinitely better.

Stage 2 – Create a New, Intimate Relationship Bond; Change Your Communication Patterns

Step 5: Both of you are now able to talk about your feelings that get triggered by the negative cycle; including things you might not have been able to say before. With less friction and more compassion between you, there is safety to explore your experience more deeply. We all have doubts about ourselves at times and may also have fears about depending on others. You may struggle with personal fears or insecurities in this relationship. You may have had life experiences that make it difficult to trust others to be there for you. With the help of your therapist, you can take turns and begin to share these "raw spots" with your partner. As you take these risks, your partner begins to truly see and understand where you are coming from, which creates empathy.

Step 6: This step involves staying engaged and listening to your partner's disclosures. Your partner may share feelings that take you by surprise. You may feel disoriented or even hurt that you have not heard your partner share so personally like this before. It is OK to experience a mixture of emotions. Start by trying to understand at an emotional level what your partner is saying, without needing to change his/her experience or take responsibility for it yourself. Stay open to the possibility of experiencing and understanding your partner in a new way. Allow yourself to be moved by your partner's new disclosures.

Step 7: Explore what helps you feel deeply connected, what is most important for you in this relationship. In this stage of therapy your therapist helps you find ways to ask for your needs in the relationship in a way that is both caring and direct. You can lean into and reach for your partner and he or she is able to reach back in a loving way. You have found a new way to relate when one of you feels stressed, hurt, or insecure. The bond between you shifts, becoming closer and more intimate. You can check out your perceptions and talk about feelings. You can listen with an open heart, be curious about one another and offer reassurance when needed. Both of you have a felt sense of "being there" for each other.

Stage 3 – Use New Communication Patterns to Solve Problems and Maintain Intimacy

Step 8: Revisit old problems or decisions that have been put on hold (e.g., parenting, finances, sex, family issues, health concerns, etc.) while staying emotionally connected. They don't seem as loaded now that you feel heard, valued, close and secure. Focus on staying accessible, responsive, and engaged while talking about practical issues. Together, you can face any of life's challenges more easily.

Step 9: Congratulations! You have reshaped your relationship. Or perhaps this is the first time in your relationship that you have felt a profound bond with one another. You have worked hard to get here, so it's important to celebrate it and put safeguards in place to protect it. Create rituals together that privilege your relationship. Find ways of keeping this new way of relating strong.

EMOTIONALLY FOCUSED THERAPY
PRACTICE GROUPS

Arrayed below is a list of the many local communities which have sprung up throughout the country supporting the practice of Emotionally Focused Therapy. Each community, and their web site, describes the process and also provides a list of local therapists who have trained in this model. Some communities, like the Maryland/DC group, boasts membership of therapists as far afield as Virginia and West Virginia, so it may be useful to check out the web sites for groups in adjoining states.

The Parent Organization, listed just below, maintains a current and comprehensive list of therapists in every state who have been trained in Emotionally Focused Therapy. The training at this point is a step-step process.

Step One is a four day "Externship," in which therapists are introduced to EFT, its theoretical foundation and the carefully constructed steps of the therapy process.
Step Two is an eight-day "Core Skills" training which is limited in enrollment and offered two or three times per year in various locations throughout the U.S. and Canada. Therapists meet four times for two-days each and learn the model in greater depth.
Step Three is the final step toward "Certification" as an EFT therapist. This step, as described on the ICEEFT web site, involves many hours of review of recordings of actual therapy sessions with a supervisor. This process concludes with demonstration, through video recordings of mastery of the steps of EFT.

Visits to the web sites, below, along with the descriptions of EFT on the individual websites of many practitioners will give insight into the enthusiasm and commitment that has been ignited in the couples therapy community.

Parent Organization
International Centre For Excellence in Emotionally Focused Therapy: http://www.iceeft.com

Arizona
AZ-EFT Community: http://www.azeft.com

California
Northern California Community for Emotionally Focused Therapy:
http://www.ncceft.com
The Orange County Community for Emotionally Focused Therapy:
http://wwwtrieft.org
The Greater Sacramento Davis EFT Community: http://sacdeft.org
L.A. Center for Emotionally Focused Therapy: http://www.laceft.org

Colorado
Colorado Center for Emotionally Focused Therapy:
http://www.coloradoeft.com
Boulder Community for Emotionally Focused Therapy:
http://www.bouldereft.com
Denver Community for Emotionally Focused Therapists:
http://www.denvereftcommunity.com

Georgia
EFT Atlanta: http://eftatlanta.com

Illinois
Chicago Center for Emotionally Focused Therapy:
http://chicagoeft.com

Kentucky
Tennessee Kentucky Center for Emotionally Focused Therapy:
http://efttennessee.com

Maryland
Maryland/DC Center for EFT:
http://washingtonbaltimorecenterforeft.com

New England
New England Community for EFT:
http://newenglandeftcommunity.com

New Jersey
New Jersey Center for Emotionally Focused Therapy:
http://www.njceft.com

New York
New York Center for Emotionally Focused Therapy:
http://www.nyceft.org

North Carolina
Greensboro Charlotte Center for EFT: http://gcceft.com

Oregon
Oregon Community for EFT: http://www.eftoregon.com

Pennsylvania
Philadelphia Center for Emotionally Focused Therapy:
http://www.philadelphiacenterforeft.org

Tennessee
Tennessee Kentucky Center for Emotionally Focused Therapy:
http://efttennessee.com

Texas
Houston EFT: http://www.eftzone.com

Utah
EFT Salt Lake City: http://www.eftslc.com

Virginia
Maryland/DC Center for EFT:
http://washingtonbaltimorecenterforeft.com

Washington
Seattle Community for Emotionally Focused Therapy:
http://seattleeft.com

ADDITIONAL RESOURCES FOR THOSE SEEKING COUPLES THERAPY

GENERAL
American Association of Marriage and Family Therapists:
www.aamft.org

National Registry of Marriage Friendly Therapists:
https://www.marriagefriendlytherapists.com/

THE GOTTMAN APPROACH
The Gottman Institute: https://www.gottman.com/
The Seven Principles for Making Marriage Work by John Gottman and Nan Silver

IMAGO THERAPY/HARVILLE HENDRIX
Imago Relationships International: https://www.imagorelationships.org/
Getting the Love You Want by Harville Hendrix

RELATIONAL LIFE THERAPY/TERRY REAL
Relational Life Institute: http://www.terryreal.com/
The New Rules of Marriage by Terrence Real

ELLYN BADER/PETER PETERSON
The Couples Institute: http://www.couplesinstitute.com/

ESTHER PEREL/RELATIONSHIPS REDEFINED
Esther Perel: http://www.estherperel.com/
Mating in Captivity by Esther Perel

STAN TATKIN'S PSYCHOGIOLOGICAL APPROACH
The PACT Institute: http://thepactinstitute.com/
Wired for Love by Stan Tatkin

DAVID SCHNARCH/CRUCIBLE THERAPY
Crucible Institute: http://crucibletherapy.com/
Passionate Marriage by David Schnarch

PRAGMATIC/EXPERIENTIAL THERAPY/BRENT ATKINSON
The Couples Clinic: http://thecouplesclinic.com/
Developing Habits for Relationship Success by Brent Atkinson

DOHERTY RELATIONSHIP INSTITUTE
Doherty Relationship Institute: http://dohertyrelationshipinstitute.com/
Take Back Your Marriage by William Doherty
Take Back Your Wedding by William Doherty and Elizabeth Doherty Thomas

DAN WILE/COLLABORATIVE COUPLES THERAPY
Collaborative Couples Therapy: http://danwile.com/
After the Honeymoon by Dan Wile

About the Author

Joseph Shaub has been an *attorney* for more than forty years and *marriage and family therapist* for more than twenty. Since arriving in Seattle from Southern California in 1995, he has been a popular columnist for both lawyer and therapist publications in the Pacific Northwest and is a sought-after speaker. His many workshops, including *Family Law for the Mental Health Professional; The Psychology of Divorce; Confidentiality, Privilege and Recordkeeping for Therapists;* and *Basic* and *Advanced Training in Collaborative Law* have been mainstays in the Northwest Community. Joe and his wife can either be found hiking local trails or reading by the fireside, depending on the season. Their daughter is pursuing a graduate degree in nutrition policy and they eat frequently to test her theories.

All inquiries and comments are welcome.
Contact joe@josephshaub.com.

You are invited to visit Joe's website: www.josephshaub.com.

Made in the USA
Charleston, SC
14 April 2016